ENDORSEMENTS

As pastor of Grace Fellowship Church, I had the honor of having Daniel Amstutz become our first full-time worship leader. He and Tracy served for eight years, and Daniel's heart and style of worship "spoiled" us. I used to tell him he did not lead us into the presence of God, he "yanked" us into the presence of God. From the moment He began worship, the presence of God could be felt. His book, *The Place of His Presence*, explains why. He knows his covenant, his relationship with Jesus, his union with Tracy and with the Body of Christ. This is the foundation for his worship relationship with the Father. His worship truly comes from the inside and is lived out of his life. After reading this book, your worship can too. It's a great book.

BOB YANDIAN
President of Bob Yandian Ministries

I've known Daniel Amstutz for at least 30 years and have been greatly impacted by his life and ministry, personally and professionally. I was privileged to serve for several years as a musician in the orchestra at Grace Fellowship in Tulsa, Oklahoma, where Daniel was the worship pastor. These were formative years for me as a worship leader, songwriter and producer.

In addition to being a great worship leader, Daniel is a gifted administrator and team builder, empowering and encouraging those he leads. He's a man of integrity, has a humble heart, he's a faithful friend, and is the same person on

stage or off stage. I highly recommend Daniel and his new ministry, Daniel Amstutz Collective, to you.

DON MOEN
President
Don Moen Productions

I've known Daniel for a few years now. He is consistent on stage as he is when he's off the stage. Daniels new book, *The Place of His Presence*, is not just another book on worship. You will find new wine in this new writing as rhythms of grace take over your soul and reposition you to your true image and what you have in Christ. The limitless possibility of having a 24/7 face-to-face experience with God Himself in worship.

JEROME FERNANDO
General overseer of KRC/PJFM
www.prophetjerome.com

THE PLACE

OF HIS

PRESENCE

THE PLACE

OF HIS

PRESENCE

Awakening to the Life and Spirit Within

DANIEL AMSTUTZ

Published by Harrison House Publishers
Shippensburg, PA 17257

Cover design by Eileen Rockwell
Interior design by Terry Clifton

ISBN 13 TP: 978-1-6803-1687-2
ISBN 13 eBook: 978-1-6803-1688-9
ISBN 13 HC: 978-1-6803-1690-2
ISBN 13 LP: 978-1-6803-1689-6

For Worldwide Distribution, Printed in the U.S.A.
1 2 3 4 5 6 7 8 / 25 24 23 22 21

CONTENTS

FOREWORD   *by Rick Renner* 1

FOREWORD   *by Andrew Wommack* 3

INTRODUCTION   It's Just a Matter of Time .5

1   Image Produces Identity 17

2   The Worshiper's Image. 55

3   Divine Appointments Defy Social Barriers 77

4   Perspective Changes Everything 99

5   There's Something About Daily Life 123

6   It's Not Complicated 145

7   Your Heart Matters. 167

8   Dying to the Natural, Living in the Supernatural . . 187

9   Being Filled. 205

10   The Unforced Rhythms of Grace 223

Closing Prayer for a New Beginning. 247

FOREWORD

Thirty years ago, Daniel Amstutz set out to write a book on worship, but it was premature for its time. But now the time for *The Place of His Presence* has arrived. Like water on a fire that boils to the surface, this book has been percolating in Daniel's heart for decades. This remarkable work has boiled up from deep within his spirit into amazing material that is hot with the presence of God.

As I read all ten chapters, I kept exclaiming, "This is amazing!" "This is *brilliant*." "This is one of the best books I've ever read!" "This is the most comprehensive thing I've ever read on the subject of worship." *The Place of His Presence* is not only filled with revelatory truth, but it is jam-packed with stories you need to hear. Daniel's decades in ministry and his wealth of relationships with people when they were unknown and later became *well* known is simply remarkable. He shares priceless treasures of wisdom from his experiences with those famous worship leaders and songwriters in the pages of this book.

From beginning to end, I was captivated, and I'm sure you will be too. You will richly benefit from Daniel's unique, personal, and delightful style of writing that goes right to the heart.

Yes, I am a personal friend of Daniel, but I am also a wholehearted fan. That is why I enthusiastically recommend this book and encourage you to make it a priority to read it from cover to cover!

RICK RENNER
Author, Teacher, Pastor, Broadcaster
Moscow, Russia

FOREWORD

Daniel Amstutz has been a personal friend for over three decades. I've known him as the music director at multiple churches and I've been with him when he pastored a church. He has traveled with me as far back as the '80s when we only had a handful of people come to the meetings. Now he directs all the praise and worship at our Charis Bible College in Woodland Park Colorado where we pack out our 3200-seat auditorium.

Like anyone who has been in ministry for 50 years, Daniel has certainly had his share of challenges. Back in 2008 we went to lunch together and he shared with me his desire to get back into ministry. For a number of years he had to revert to faux painting to support his family and he had a very success-ful business, but his heart was clearly in the music ministry. I prayed and agreed with him, not realizing at the time that I was also affecting my future.

Daniel came on staff at Charis Bible College in 2011 and has taken not only the music ministry but the whole Bible college to another level. Our praise and worship is some of the best anywhere and he is able to bridge the generation gaps that exist between our younger and older students. Daniel has produced five music CDs with his Charis Worship which are some of my favorites.

Daniel also leads our third-year worship track where he trains our students not only in music quality but in the heart of worship. Daniel has a revelation on New Testament worship that glorifies the finished work of Christ instead of begging God for what He has already done.

Daniel also leads our healing school which meets every Thursday. He has trained thousands of prayer ministers on how to teach and minister healing to others. We have thousands of testimonies of healing through the healing school and many more through the students who have graduated and gone on to share these truths with others. Daniel also leads our Healing is Here conference every summer with thousands of healings reported at each conference.

All of this is to say that Daniel is a seasoned minister with proven results and he knows what he's talking about. I've seen and experienced the fruit he produces and it's good. I highly recommend Daniel and his new book, *The Place of His Presence.* If it does for you what it's done for Daniel, you will be mightily blessed and better able to know the Lord and make Him known.

ANDREW WOMMACK
President of Andrew Wommack Ministries
Founder and President of Charis Bible College

IT'S JUST A MATTER OF TIME

I started writing a book on worship for a major publisher in 1989—and sadly never finished it. It wasn't completed for several very good reasons, not the least of which was being busy traveling in ministry. It ended up on the back burner, with the intention of getting to it as soon as I could find time. I never found it. I never made time for it!

At that time in my life as a songwriter and recording artist, I had recorded two solo projects and five live worship projects. I also held seminars and was a guest speaker at large worship gatherings all around the world.

Trying to be a blessing to as many people as possible, I moved from one state to another. Then I moved from an international stage of ministry presence and influence to a new season of mostly unintended obscurity. My traveling ministry became a fraction of what it once was, as leadership responsibilities in a smaller church became more demanding and diverse. Compared to the focus I had been used to for nearly a decade, I nevertheless grew so much spiritually during this time. And as always, God worked all things together for good, as He does so well!

Eventually two more moves were made to two more states, both for ministry reasons. When the end of the 1990s approached and 1999 became "Y2K," it was sadly and even falsely prophesied by some as "the end of the world." But amazingly, another morning arrived, as did another day, another year, another decade, and life went on. The "non-prophets" made their necessary adjustments, and so did I.

A wiser, older mentor once told me through the changing seasons of life, and especially through the unexpected storms of life, that I could either be bitter or get better. Even though I knew I didn't want to be bitter, I wasn't sure how to do the latter. As a worshiper, I knew being bitter was not a good option. I knew it would be toxic for my heart, thus defiling my life; but what I didn't know yet was how "getting better" was not about self-improvement. I was learning to live under a better covenant with better promises, and I was about to discover a better way to worship and a better way to live life.

Years later, one cold, snowy winter morning in Colorado I was looking through my original notes from the first twelve chapters of what I had written back in 1989. I must confess, I was so glad that book had not been published. I have grown and matured spiritually since then, and I could see how much that growth had changed my thinking. It's not that what I had written was in error or "off the wall" doctrinally; but being much more destination focused in my younger years, I hadn't yet come to appreciate the journey as much as I do now. I realized that not only was I in a new geographical location, but my heart was in a new place as well—a place of much more grace, amazing grace and abundant grace.

REVELATION OF WORSHIP

A few years after graduation from college, when I started in worship ministry, it was very difficult to find any helpful books on worship or worship ministry; at least, that was my perception. I sure didn't realize it then, but I know now that what I wanted was confirmation for the "new wineskin" that I saw and heard from the Holy Spirit. Formation was happening inside me, but I was still passionately seeking confirmation around me! What I did find in a library usually seemed so out of date and irrelevant and was usually more historical, which certainly has a place. But that was where I had been; it wasn't the place where I wanted to go! I was being shown something that was new to me. I stepped out in faith, trusting that what I was hearing was really from God—and it's been an amazing journey!

As the revelation of worship exploded in the church in the 1970s and early '80s, so did the communication of that revelation. It seemed like "all of a sudden" there were new songs, new ideas, and new books coming from everywhere about worship—let alone new seminars, workshops, and eventually even new "how to" VHS videos instructing anyone who might be interested in anything musical. There was everything from how to play that new popular song on the keyboard or guitar just like the original, to how to correctly dance in church, or make banners that would guarantee the presence of Jesus to show up!

In the 1990s when the internet became a tool of communication, informational overload began. This was long before today's reality with nearly everyone having a smartphone and access to instant information.

As is often the case, what started off genuinely birthed by the Holy Spirit as informational, revelational, and even transformational over time became mostly "inspirational," even with worship.

Even by the 1990s, let alone now, major recording labels and companies specialized in "all things worship" as well as an abundance of new music. There were and are so many books and online options that we became inundated and overwhelmed with all the new and the resulting options. It became acceptable practice for worship teams to get the latest top 40 worship songs and do their best to "imitate" what was being made popular and acceptable. It seemed logical that if it was already successful, then you and your team would be too!

> **What started as revelation was replaced by imitation!**

At first, it was as if no one really noticed; but in many places, the same songs were being sung, even though the songs and the church doctrines were often completely opposing each other. I often say now, "If you wouldn't teach it from the pulpit, then don't teach it in a psalm, a hymn, or a spiritual song!" The Baptists, Episcopalians, and even Catholics were singing some of the same songs as the Foursquare and Assembly of God churches. Worship became categorized as either "contemporary" or "traditional."

At first, I think most of us on worship teams or involved in church worship were very happy about the songs bringing what looked like unity. We were happy about it all, because we were experiencing numerical growth, which was the whole point, right? Even though we didn't realize it yet, over time I believe that worship was being shaped more by surveys and public opinion than by the Spirit of God. Unity only comes from the Holy Spirit working through the love of God, not by our songs. Unintentionally, in many cases, instead of being dominated by God's opinion, worship started to become more about "style" than substance.

A battle for generational ground had quietly begun on the back of the pews. Hymnbooks and overhead projectors collided—and who was right? Like a slow fade on an LP, style and substance, reality and truth, and even technology and tradition were all there competing for the last word. But despite this competition, there was something pure and authentic in it all that was not going away.

Old wineskins can never hold new wine, nor can new wine be poured back into old wineskins. We knew that, right?

In Mark 2:21-22, Jesus says, *"No one sews a piece of unshrunk cloth on an old garment; or else the new piece pulls away from the old, and the tear is made worse."* I believe this is what happened when the veil was torn in two when Jesus died on the cross. The new covenant had pulled away from the old and the veil being torn in two was the result. Something new was being birthed. *"And no one puts new wine into old wineskins; or else the new wine bursts the wineskins, the wine is spilled, and the wineskins are ruined. But new wine must be put into new wineskins."*

New and old were clashing again just like here in the gospel. This new clash wasn't the music, even though we thought it was; the clash was about the covenants! Instead of "Spirit-filled worship" or "worship in spirit and truth" or something that had the power of His presence, sadly I saw and heard much of our public worship start to become a form—but denying the power thereof. It was "style filled" but not necessarily "Spirit filled."

The lifestyle of worship in our daily lives didn't seem to be connecting with the public during our weekly gatherings; or was it? Maybe that *was* what was happening! Were we still trying to perform and please? Was the absence of a personal revelation of grace becoming the public norm? What would Jesus do?

It seemed to be more about the music, the excellence, and being relevant! Leaders everywhere were giving people what was popular, and why not? Who in their right mind would *choose* to be culturally out of touch or do what had already been done?

At first everyone wanted something different and something that was "as good as what they were seeing on TV." Instead of God's Word being the standard, many leaders started imitating what was creatively being done on television, as if this was the accepted standard. What was God's perspective on the typical weekend gathering? Who were we gathering for, exactly?

Excellence often led to entertainment; the "us and them" started to become normal. The consumer was becoming "the commander," the one calling the shots—even "the demander." And if your church couldn't deliver, they would find a place that would, and the pressure was on to build the church through customer service, as discipleship seemed to be swallowed up by opinion and options.

But wait a minute! We knew worship is vital, so why couldn't worship build up the church?

At first that logic seemed right; but worship doesn't build the church—*Jesus does!* Only Jesus is qualified to build the church because the church is supernatural, and Jesus is the only One worthy to head up the building program! Jesus builds and worship responds!

Ephesians 5:23 describes Jesus: *"Christ is head of the church."* What is *He* saying? What is God's perspective? If *we* try to build people through style and behavior modification (in the natural), we will eventually become a powerless "church" substituting the authentic (the supernatural realm) for a cheap imitation of what was intended; the result will be form with no power.

Opinion only saw "a carpenter's Son," but faith saw the Father's only begotten Son!

As consumer attitude increased, finding a place where the worship was to one's standard and style seemed to become the most important factor of all. In an effort to grow and be effective, the lyrics of many songs reflected the need to be relevant, and many adapted to lyrics that were often more poetic than scriptural.

Ancient and modern were colliding as if in slow motion. Contemporary and traditional became like opposing teams on the football field. Inspiration was replacing revelation, and many in the 21st century church started to get inoculated with a toxic mixture of what was comfortable, popular, and even financially profitable. Big business was replacing Kingdom business!

Some started rewriting the Word of God to fit their perspective and, in reality, started developing "another gospel" that was more about *them* than God, more about humanism than the God who loves humanity! Think about it though—the gospel that they had been exposed to was in word only, if at all, and rarely were they teaching the Word of God in "power and demonstration of the Holy Spirit" or with signs and wonders following. Who even knew what that was? There is no substitute for the Holy Spirit!

In an effort to leave nothing out, they put everything in!

Others in leadership were not going to ignore the Word of God, but as if being mentored by a mad chemist, they began to develop toxic combinations of the Old and the New Covenants, teaching law and grace and presenting that combination as the new normal.

Instead of seeing the goodness of God being exalted, we saw the exploitation of the "goodness of humans"—and it wasn't good!

Instead of seeing how the New Covenant was the fulfillment of the Old Covenant and learning from the examples given to us by God in the Old Covenant, many worshipers were becoming more and more confused, as the toxic combinations became acceptable practice; mega spiritual dysfunction was the result. So much "dys" function from the original blueprint of what I believe God had in mind for us led to a generation where many are now disconnected, disillusioned, and disappointed. There is a lot of "dys and dat" in the church today as a result. The original recipe was getting replaced with a dash of dys and a little of dat, many times resulting in a dysfunctional, counterfeit gospel. For some, the "good news" was becoming bad news! What God had called good many were calling evil.

Young worshipers were often ignorant of God's Word, establishing their own patterns of what was comfortable for them. Older worshipers were often performing for God's approval with perfect church attendance and never missing the giving of a tithe so that they wouldn't be cursed with a curse by the God they were trying to love.

Trying to do everything just right, people were growing more and more exhausted in the process; Jesus said His burden was light and easy, and what we were experiencing didn't seem that way at all. Most of the time it was heavy and hard, and we were growing weary, but who would dare say that? The counterfeit invention of our own dysfunction, stemming from a lack of knowledge, was heavy and making everyone around us weary!

As is always the case, method slowly began to replace revelation, mystery, and wonder; and just in case the "Holy Spirit didn't show up," it was only wisdom to be prepared and have a plan, don't you know! After all, those of us in leadership were responsible for "bringing in the presence of God" on our shoulders, or so we wrongly believed (Old Covenant thinking).

At first it seemed right, but the problem was that as a kingdom of priests, we would never find our true identity "on our shoulders" but rather "on our knees" from inside our new hearts (New Covenant thinking)!

There were all these concepts that older folks would sometimes talk about like the "fear of the Lord" or "speaking in tongues" or "the anointing that broke yokes," and for many of the younger generation these were just some outdated phrases from weird people. Something must have died off somewhere down the line, like maybe with the last apostle! Yeah, that's it! We were modern people and after all we were educated and somewhat sophisticated—maybe even professional. Thank You anyway, Jesus, but we got this!

Not too long ago, early one morning somewhere at the intersection of sleep and awake, I clearly heard the Holy Spirit remind me of the book that I started writing in 1989, and even though that moment in time had come and gone, I felt the Holy Spirit saying that the time had come to write a new book. A new book on what He had been showing me about worship, what He was speaking to my heart, and what I had learned as a result! Writing a book on worship has since been confirmed by so many people who didn't know each other, so many times, and on so many occasions, that it became embarrassing.

For so long, it was hard to imagine ever finishing that book on worship that I started in the 1980s or, frankly, even write a new one! Because of all the books that had already been written on worship, and all the information that is now available on the internet, I thought to myself that the last thing we needed was another book on worship. But something was different this time. Something new and urgent was coming together in me, and I knew it was the fullness of time for me to write this book. I felt compelled to share my heart, realizing a new generation would never benefit from something not communicated.

I know now that the calling on my life includes putting into writing what He has personally shown me by the Holy Spirit, as well as what I've been taught by many wonderful leaders. I've written so many songs, so many sermons, a lot of curriculum for college courses, and so many notes over the years, but I've never written a book. I know now that this is not just to fulfill a heart's desire—even though it did become one and has grown into a big one—but it is a step of obedience out of my love for God and for you! I have to pass on to the next generation what God has shown me!

However, I need to give a disclaimer, and it is this: I do not pretend for a moment to be an expert on this subject or to have a corner on the market of knowing all about worship. In fact, the longer I have lived and the more I have grown in God, the more I realize what I don't know. It's just a matter of time!

Thank God we have an eternity together where we will know even as we are known. Every ministry on earth is going to cease except one—worship will continue forever! God is love and love never fails. Love will always, always find expression in earth and in heaven. The best is yet to come!

1

IMAGE PRODUCES IDENTITY

WHAT'S NEW?

We often greet each other with the phrase, "Hey, what's new?" What's new? How about—everything! Second Corinthians 5:17 says, *"Therefore, if anyone is in Christ, he is a new creation; old things have passed away; behold, all things have become new."*

I have traveled quite a bit in my life and have moved way too many times, both as the son of a Baptist pastor and as a minister myself. I have been sound asleep and either had to get up to use the restroom or been suddenly awakened only to realize I had no idea where I was. What a strange feeling to not know what city you're in or why you are in a hotel bed. Who moved that bed anyway from the location that you were used to? Why is the bathroom suddenly on the wrong side of the room? Who changed the place!?

Upon returning home after our honeymoon in 1977, I remember waking up in my Colorado apartment with a woman in my bed! Not being fully awake, I remember feeling a strange mixture of panic and confusion as to why there was a woman in bed with me. After a few seconds of "singles time warp"—even though it felt more like minutes while trying to come to grips with this new season—I was so relieved when I realized I was married; it was legal, it was godly, and it was new. We enjoyed a good belly laugh over that moment and learned that "new" required change. Tracy and I had established a new covenant together and "two became one." Her location changed and she moved in with me, changing my location from the inside out. Later that week, one of my friends just making casual conversation said, "Hey bro, what's new?" I answered, "Everything!"

Something supernatural happened by the Holy Spirit when we were joined together in marriage, as two believers becoming one "in Christ," that was beyond the material or physical world. Two individuals spiritually became one in unity, purpose, and fulfilled destiny. And now as a team of two distinct personalities and opposites in many ways, we began to discover on a daily basis that we had much more than a legal contract; it was a covenant relationship! Not only was life going to be different for her while learning how to be a wife, but for me as well. My life was changed for the better by marrying Tracy—way better!

The covenant of marriage demanded a change of location for both of us! It was no longer her dorm room and my apartment—it was no longer hers and mine—now it was ours. We came together, and by doing so established something new.

Not only was there a change in my physical location, there was a change of location in my heart that affected my thought life, my emotions, my attitudes, even my perceptions and goals. Really, everything changed. Okay, even my closet space and especially my bathroom!

According to the Bible in John 3:16, we learn that God *so* loved the world that He gave His only Son. Something powerful and intimate is revealed when we see the love of God expressed within the Godhead, the mysterious "Three in One." We see how God the Father loves the Son and how the Holy Spirit loves to exalt Jesus; we also see then how Jesus loves the church and gave Himself for the church.

I am so grateful that by God's grace I was able to see from *this image* how I can love my wife as *Christ loved the church,* giving myself to her and serving her, and because of God's grace my wife could submit to me as her husband *as unto the Lord* without the fear of being controlled or abused. In love, we could submit one to another and live to give! Because each of our spiritual identities was "in Christ" as believers, we had common ground to build our marriage.

> The image of "Christ and the church" produced a supernatural identity in our marriage.

I am blessed to tell you that as of this writing we are celebrating our 42nd year of marriage, and somehow we are more in love with each other than ever. Shortly after our engagement, Tracy gave me a picture that she made in an art class while majoring in elementary education in college, showing an image of a bucket being lowered into a well, and at the bottom of the picture she wrote, "As He gives to me, I give to you." I treasure that to this day! What more could I want? God as our limitless Source? Yes, please!

GRACE FOUND A PLACE

God wanted something more for us than what the people of the Old Covenant had—something much more! He wanted *us* and knew that in the fullness of time a location change would be required for Him to see His joy be our strength. What was *His joy?*

It's certainly no secret that one of the most fundamental differences between the Old and the New Covenants is location. As sinners, we were a world apart from God. We were separated with no way of coming together as one. When God the Father sent His only Son, Jesus, *everything changed!*

The Word became flesh and was living among us on planet Earth! Jesus—the Way, the Truth, and the Life—physically lived on earth and showed us how no one comes to the Father except through Him. He already was the Word of God; but now, by the Holy Spirit, the timeless Word stepped into time to become Jesus. He changed location in order to destroy the works of the devil, become our perfect sacrifice, and show us the Father (1 John 3:8). Think of it. He changed location because of love. Jesus wanted you and me to be with Him forever and gave His life to make it happen. It appears we are a big deal to God.

We are the joy set before Him that helped Him endure the cross. He didn't endure the cross for His sake. The thought of us becoming brand-new creations, and thereby being with Him for eternity, was joy enough for Jesus to endure that horrible death and that "wonderful cross"! The Lord's joy was relationship with us. We will talk more about this later.

What incredible love! Greater love has no one than to lay down our lives for our friends (John 15:13). Was Jesus really calling us "friends"?

Having a relationship with God in spirit and truth is the only way we can have a relationship with the God who is Spirit! This is the foundational meaning of being a true worshiper. Because He came here and made Himself available in a human body, He became the ultimate sacrifice for our sin! He was sinless, so in taking our place, dying our death, and becoming the curse for us our location changed as a result.

> **This divine exchange is available to anyone, but it is not automatic to everyone.**

Through faith we were given the opportunity to receive by grace what Jesus did for us. When He died, we died. When He arose from the dead, we arose in Him. When He sat down on the right hand of the Majesty on High, we sat down in Him.

We must believe and receive what God provided for us in Christ. Now for the first time in history, as human beings, *we are allowed to be the place of His presence.* We are not waiting on God to provide. He is waiting on us to receive. We enter into the finished work of Jesus by faith, receiving what He has already given by grace.

Through Christ, God's grace found a new place. It was His idea. The presence of God that used to just come upon people was about to move from outside to inside. Immanuel, God with us, was about to become Christ in us, the hope of glory. What amazing grace!

NEW LOCATION REQUIRED NEW ACCOMMODATION

In the Old Covenant, the worshiper would have to go to a place to worship, but in the New Covenant something unheard of was about to be revealed in that we would become the place of worship. We will unpack this truth together in this book, but still today the epic lack of knowledge about this reality is tragic.

As worshipers who we have become the place of His presence, where His Spirit abides, why are we still trying so hard to get to a place to worship? Why are we still putting ourselves under an Old Covenant by thinking we have to go to a place to worship, instead of gathering together as worshipers? Why are we seeking His presence as if we don't have it?

Jesus said He came to fulfill the Old Covenant and remove the veils that were separating us once and for all (Luke 24:44; Matthew 27:51). New accommodation had already been made by God Himself, even though many in Jesus' day didn't recognize it. Many in our day don't realize that there is a new temple either. They don't know that God's desire is for them to be the place of His presence; they too don't realize that right now "new living temples" are all over the face of the earth. Once you know the veil has been removed in Christ, why would you ever want to go back to an empty form with no power?

Worshiping through a veil is the most frustrating way to try to worship. No more veils, please!

So who changed the place, you ask? Jesus did, once and for all. This change of location becomes a "Good News Headline" to be shouted from the rooftops. It's bigger than big. It's epic!

Realizing and receiving this change of location will change you!

In the business of real estate, the number-one saying heard over and over is, "Location, location, location!" I remember thinking to myself, *What does that mean?* It means that identical properties can increase or decrease in value due to location. God had such value on you, as a person, a human being, because of the finished work of Jesus on the cross and His resurrection. The time had finally come for Him not just to be with you, but to move in. No longer was He going to relate to us and try to impact our hearts from the outside in.

It was the fullness of time, and from now on it was going to be about a New Covenant. Jesus said the time had come when what had been hidden for centuries as a mystery to the wisest of the wise was now to be revealed at the appointed time.

You and I are living in that appointed time of a location change!

Only because of Jesus, all who believed and received were about to become God's home. He was finally moving into His new place—His very own living room.

GOD WANTS YOU

Ephesians 1:13-14 says, *"In Him you also trusted, after you heard the word of truth, the gospel of your salvation; in whom also, having believed, you were sealed with the Holy Spirit of promise, who is the guarantee of our inheritance until the redemption of the purchased possession, to the praise of His glory."*

God wants what He paid for! Your salvation was free to you, but it cost Him everything.

Romans 12:1 (ESV) tells us, *"I appeal to you therefore, brothers, by the mercies of God, to present your bodies as a living sacrifice, holy and acceptable to God, which is your spiritual worship."*

And 1 Corinthians 6:19-20 (ESV) says, *"Or do you not know that your body is a temple of the Holy Spirit within you, whom you have from God? You are not your own, for you were bought with a price. So glorify God in your body."*

Paul tells us in 1 Corinthians 12:27 (ESV), *"Now you are the body of Christ and individually members of it."*

God wants to live life in you and through you. God wants you to be His place of grace! He moved in you by His Spirit, and God is jealous over you.

As the body of Christ, we must see ourselves through the eyes of the Lord Jesus—and we can do that only through the Word of God. How many times have we prayed the Ephesians' prayer that the eyes of our heart or our understanding would be opened so that we can see what we need to see (Ephesians 1:18). When we see ourselves as God sees us, then and only then will we begin to see the world through His eyes.

> **Knowing you are loved by God leads to passion for His presence, leading to compassion for all people.**

We must also have an ear to hear what God is saying to us personally as well as what He wants us to hear for others. We can then boldly declare His good news from the rooftops. If we are not seeing, hearing, and learning to be alert and aware within our new identity in Christ, we will be completely out of touch with what is happening in the world around us—the world that God so loves.

God is working mightily in us to love unconditionally through us; His love is communicated primarily through our thoughts, words, and actions. These are containers of image and identity, because every thought or word carries an image with it, which is why thoughts and words matter so much.

When an image is formed in us, it will eventually lead to identity.

Because God's Word is alive and powerful, it will lead to transformation when we believe it and receive it. Truth written by the Spirit of God will produce the image that becomes an identity, resulting in action. Once that image comes alive in us, it will affect our identity, which determines how we live our life.

Proverbs 23:7 says, *"For as he thinks in his heart, so is he."*

One of the main reasons why Jesus came to the earth, according to 1 John 3:4-10, was to destroy the works of the devil, not exalt them and call them normal. His love for us is amazing; God has always desired us to live a quality life and to know how loved we are and how good He is.

The devil is real, and he has real strategies to destroy us that are expressed in the reality of everyday life; there is a real war happening that is not a video game or just some spiritual poetic imagery (Ephesians 6:11). This is why we need to live our life *in Christ*. Jesus triumphed over the devil by dying on the cross and then rising from the dead. The devil is defeated, but he's not dead. Jesus has given us His victory! He conquered, and we now have more than conquered through Jesus!

As in the Garden of Eden, the enemy is still asking, "Did God really say…?" The devil also uses thought, image, and action to try to redefine and counterfeit anything and everything godly to make it lose its power and its strength in our lives. A little leaven leavens the whole thing (Galatians 5:9).

The devil is the loser, not us. It's a losing strategy to ever make sin acceptable and normal and think that there will not be any consequence for our actions. Sin is never a winning strategy!

Even though it's the enemy who steals, kills, and destroys, there is no sin that is bigger than God's love for us. He comes to bring life that is full of meaning and blessing to us through Christ.

Think of this image and identity. Greater is He who is in you than he who is in the world (1 John 4:4). God is the only One who can turn around what the devil intends for our harm and somehow bring good out of it (Romans 8:28). He loves us and wants what He paid for! His love for us has already provided forgiveness and healing! Our past doesn't have to define our future, and God knows the plans He has for us, fulfilled through Christ. He wants us to know His plans so that we can experience the will of God in our lives every day. He has an amazing future for us. What if we really believed that?

Jeremiah 29:11 says, *"For I know the thoughts that I think toward you, says the Lord, thoughts of peace and not of evil, to give you a future and a hope."*

THOUGHTS AND WORDS PRODUCE IMAGE AND IDENTITY

In the 1970s, we wrote the lyrics of our worship songs onto cellulose acetate sheets (transparencies) and then projected them on the wall of the church auditorium so that everyone could join in the new song flowing out of the hearts of people worldwide. There was so much new, so much refreshing from the presence of the Lord, and so many new songs being sung that there were no hymnals that could contain this fresh expression of God's grace. Holy Spirit-birthed songs were coming from everywhere, and the only way we knew to share them lyrically at that time was with an overhead projector. It was easy, inexpensive—in the beginning the transparencies were written with a felt tip marker—and often messy.

Have you ever noticed how thoughts come from some-where "out there" in the strangest ways at the most spiritual of times? Like when you start to worship or start to pray? Suddenly you're bombarded in your thought life with things to do, people to see, and places to go! Sometimes the thoughts are very personal and would be incredibly embarrassing if anyone else knew what thought had just crossed your mind. It's amaz-ing that God knows and loves us anyway!

At times, those thoughts can seem so innocent, but if we don't know the Word we will never know that a "contrary thought" is contrary to the will of God. Knowing the truth of God's Word enables us to take contrary thoughts captive and bring them to the obedience of Christ. Knowing the truth is what sets us free, not just knowing information. The Word of God is truth (John 17:17). If we don't know the truth, then contrary thoughts will produce a negative or destructive image that will be written on the tablet of our heart, which will deter-mine how we live life, instead of knowing the truth, which sets us free.

However, only the truth we know is the truth that will set us free. We can't speak the truth in love if we don't know the truth. Knowing the truth set forth in God's Word, the Bible, is critically important because our thoughts lead to "reasonings," which lead to strongholds in the mind that must be torn down when they are contrary to the will of God. You can build strongholds of godliness and righteousness in the same way, but you must learn to be proactive in this and not passive, otherwise, "The devil will eat your lunch and pop the bag!" as Andrew Wommack would say.

The heart will produce whatever is written on it. What are the images in your heart right now and the resulting identity you've identified with? What do you believe about yourself? Do you see yourself as the temple of the Holy Spirit or more like a cheap hotel?

According to Dr. Caroline Leaf, 75 to 90 percent of all illness is because of wrong thinking.[1] I think that fact is amazing, and I find it fulfilling and exciting to see how science is catching up with the Word of God.

However, we as the church need to catch up and step up to the Bible in this area, so that we are no longer ignorant or living out of a lack of knowledge. We must not forfeit the instruction of truth and the demonstration of the Spirit, which our children so desperately need to experience, to someone or something else! We can't afford to fall into some counterfeit teaching and live with the resulting changed identity that affects generations to come.

The presence of God is always communicated through relationship, which is why, whether we realize it or not, our thoughts, words, and actions find their expression in our personal worship and then in our public worship. How we live life affects our legacy and profoundly impacts the future of worship for generations to come. Think about it—after you're gone, what will you leave?

I'LL NEVER LEAVE YOU

Not that long ago, I was enjoying a cup of coffee in the morning, worshiping Jesus, spending time in the Word, and just being together. In time, I began reading a book that a friend had given to me months earlier, and I came to a passage that talked about how faithful God is and always will be. How that once we have received the free gift of His grace, by faith, we are joined to Him forever; and the author highlighted how nothing would cause Him to ever leave us or forsake us.

It wasn't a truth that was unfamiliar to me at all, but for some reason another layer of gratitude began to emerge from deep within me as I was reading. My heart was so thankful that eventually I was overwhelmed with emotion and tears of joy began to flow down my face while I gave thanks again that truth is always true. Even not believing the truth doesn't change it from being truth.

As I took time to remember, I began reflecting on my life and how God had been so faithful to me even when I wasn't. I could now see clearly in this place of remembering how God had remained faithful even when I didn't think He was at the time. My perspective had changed.

Memory is so powerful; we need to remember what God has done for us, and remember often. Remembering what God has done quickly leads to thanksgiving! Psalm 42 speaks of this in the life of David and how remembering helps us stay connected and encouraged even when depression is knocking on our door.

I will share more about this later, but remembering what God's already done for you positions you for connection, encouragement, and strength instead of ending up like your smartphone that you forgot to plug in and is now out of power. And if you didn't back it up properly, it will eventually run out of memory.

As I began to think about this truth of God never leaving me, His presence was overwhelming me with a sense of belonging and divine connection. I reflected back to when I received this amazing, priceless gift of God's grace at only five years old. My mother led me to Jesus, and even though I didn't understand like I do now, I knew I needed Jesus in my life. I knew I needed to know Him, not just know about Him. Now all these years later, with my cup of coffee in hand, as I began to personalize this and remember how God in Christ redeemed me and changed location not only to be with me but to live in me by the Holy Spirit, I was

He loved me as I was, not as who I was going to become.

overwhelmed with thankfulness and praise as I worshiped Him. He loved me when I was dead and lost in my sin.

While I was a freshman attending the University of Colorado in Boulder in the early '70s, after a stressful day of exams, I went to the mountains to spend some alone time with

God. I trekked to the top of this one particular mountain and started to pray and worship. Even though I was born again, I eventually started expressing, from some place deep in my heart, my desire to live filled with Him instead of living my life filled with me. I knew "me," but I wanted to know more of Him and wanted to give Him more place in my life. That day I asked to receive the baptism of the Holy Spirit.

What I read in the Bible from the book of Acts was like a Holy Spirit adventure and it sure wasn't happening in my life—and honestly, I wasn't sure it could happen!

My mom, knowing my love for music and the arts, had sent me a book several weeks earlier that she thought I would enjoy. It was Pat Boone's book titled *A New Song*. It was written not only by a famous singer and an outspoken Christian, but also someone who had received the baptism of the Holy Spirit and was very vocal about it. My godly mom felt directed by God to share this book with me. She had been praying for me to be open spiritually to what God had for me.

Over the next several weeks, I read the book, and even though I still hadn't renewed my mind to what the Bible said concerning being filled with the Holy Spirit, I did understand that if I was baptized in the Holy Spirit I would receive power to be a witness just like the book of Acts talked about. I really hoped that my life could be an effective witness of the Lord Jesus Christ, not just by attending church. I really wanted to *be* the church! I had desire but little knowledge.

Well, that day in 1970, in the beautiful mountains west of Boulder, I was gloriously baptized in the Holy Spirit with the evidence of speaking in other tongues. The presence of

God was so strong in me I felt like warm honey was being poured all through me from the top down as I was having this supernatural encounter with the Spirit of God. It was unlike anything I had ever experienced.

When I shared what had happened to me with my leaders and spiritual friends at the church I was a part of while in college, they told me I had become overemotional and opened myself up to the demonic. Through my own broken identity, I respected them and took their opinion to be of greater value than the little I thought I knew. I was devastated and confused. I was so disappointed, disillusioned, and eventually became disconnected.

I didn't handle it well at all and made inner vows that later had to be broken off my heart. I decided that if what I experienced was demonic, then maybe I really didn't know God like I thought I did. Out of anger and in rebellion, I began to do all the things I had been taught not to do. My values shifted almost overnight. I allowed my friendship with the world to become bigger and have a place of prominence in my life, even though I maintained an appearance or an image externally of what a believer "should be" while continuing to be involved in music at this same church.

I lived a double life as "an unbelieving believer." I was trying to be conformed to the world and transformed at the same time. Once the door was open, I thought I had been lied to by my parents and the Christ followers who had been part of my life up to that point. I began to discover that sin didn't seem that bad, and in fact it was pleasurable. I hadn't quite arrived at the "for a season" part yet. At first, it was really fun and seemed to confirm what I had always wondered about the "other side." Out of my broken image I started to think differently about everything. I was trying so hard to fit in. I thought God would just distance Himself from me, but instead of leaving me or forsaking me, God kept pursuing me!

Here's what I think is so amazing about God's love—all the brokenness in my heart that was becoming my new reality and the rebellious things that I submitted to during this sad season, I did while being born again and baptized in the Holy Spirit.

Think about this with me for a minute. Jesus never left me; the Holy Spirit never left me, and yet, while God Himself was living in me, I was choosing to allow my body, the temple of the Holy Spirit, to be used to do things and go places that I knew were wrong. Why didn't the Holy Spirit just leave? Why didn't His love give up on me? Why didn't my rebellion and my brokenness drive Him away from me? Because He is all knowing, why did He remain with "damaged goods"? I wasn't worthy; someone else was much more deserving of His presence.

My whole life I had been told that I was supposed to love God with my whole heart, and I knew I wasn't doing that, but He kept loving me with His! He never changed His faithful promises to me because of my unfaithfulness.

God's love for the whole world is HIS story, literally "HIStory" in the making. God's love is so extravagant, so unchanging, so faithful. What kind of God would love me in my mess and confusion? Only God the Father, Maker of heaven and earth.

You know your own story better than anyone and things about yourself that you might never share with anyone else. However, God knows them too and loves you unconditionally, in spite of it all. What kind of God loves us even while we are spiritually dead and lost in our sin? Who else but Jesus!

The Bible says in Hebrews 11:25 that it is possible to enjoy the pleasures of sin "for a season." Thankfully that season for me was a short one, largely because of the faithful prayers of my parents, especially my mother. She was already Spirit filled at the time and recognized what had happened to me during this rebellious period of my life. She spent hours praying for me and my four siblings, as well as many others. She sent me handwritten letters pleading for me to repent and give my heart back to God. Each would usually begin with "Greetings in the wonderful name of Jesus." Because of my hardened heart, I would get so mad just reading her greeting that I would often crumple them up and throw them across the room in a wad of anger and frustration. I didn't want to hear what she had to say because I knew it was what God had to say, and trying to hear His voice was what got me into all this trouble in the first place, or so I thought!

I began to distance myself from my family and even from believing friends who had been close friends, as I tried harder and harder to become friends with the world and comfortable with my new lifestyle of sin. Even though I was already spiritually alive, it was like I was trying to be dead again. I was having an identity crisis, because of valuing the wrong image.

Years later, one of my pastors said that when a believer tries to live like an unbeliever it's like putting a living body on the cold slab next to the dead ones in the morgue, and expecting to blend in. As my wife would say, "That's just creepy!"

Even though Mom "moved to heaven" in 1993, I am still overcome with gratitude for the sacrifices she made on my behalf, but especially for the prayers she prayed. I am so grateful that those effective, fervent prayers went into my future and don't have an expiration date! I would do anything now just to have even one of those letters that I crumpled up, just as a reminder of how biblical-believing prayer really does avail much.

I was given her Bible after she passed, and it is a great treasure to me—the same Bible she prayed out of for me, with all the markings and personal notes, handwritten next to verses that spoke to her, accompanied by stain marks from tears and time. This is the Bible that I now pray out of for my family—priceless!

I have heard it said, "Sin makes you stay longer than you want to stay, go farther than you want to go, and costs more than you want to pay." I'm not proud of it, but I can tell you I personally discovered this to be true.

I went to parties, drank alcohol, and experimented with some entry-level drugs popular in the early '70s that were available on the very liberal campus in those days. I was trying so hard to be cool and have a good time. We did have some "good times," but it annoyed me how everyone was getting high and having fun, while I would see a vision or hear God calling me. Or I would be reminded of a song that held a special place in my heart about His love for me. On multiple occasions, Scripture came to me even while I was high. Why didn't He just leave me alone? Why did He keep tearing down the walls I was trying so hard to build around my heart?

His love was greater than my sin! God loved me more than the devil hated me! God kept pursuing me, even in my brokenness, and what I thought was fun became nothing but more brokenness. And the "pleasure of sin" turned to more dissatisfaction, discontentment, and disappointment. It took a couple of years, but eventually it wasn't fun anymore!

A word of advice—never try to outrun a praying mama on her knees!

YOU CAN RUN BUT YOU CAN'T HIDE

Psalm 139:7 says, *"Where can I go from Your Spirit? Or where can I flee from Your presence?"*

Not only do you know this story, but you know the ending as well, because I finally repented, which means I changed my direction. Through repentance I changed direction! In my brokenness, I received my forgiveness that had already been provided on the cross of Christ 2,000 years earlier.

Even though I was already forgiven, I still had to believe it, receive it, and make it mine. As a result, I was also able to forgive those who meant well but spoke their "human doctrines" into my life. Incredibly, I found amazing grace in my time of need, setting me free from the bondage of sin and I knew it! Something was very different!

Hebrews 4:16 says, *"Let us therefore come boldly to the throne of grace, that we may obtain mercy and find grace to help in time of need.*" I found supernatural course correction in my time of need, and I changed direction as a result.

In a Holy Spirit moment, a "supernatural suddenly," God healed my heart, restored my life. Even though I still had to daily walk it out, it was as if everything was connected inside again! The sun was brighter; I could see more clearly; my life felt clean!

God's grace still amazes me and always will! I will never get over being forgiven! The Holy Spirit kept living in my spirit the whole time I was living for myself, for my pleasure, and doing my thing. I know now, by repentance and receiving my forgiveness, something in my soul had changed, as if a barricade had been removed between my spirit and my soul. My body even responded to my decision to repent despite what my rebellion and my resistance to the things of God had put it through! God had to do some serious temple maintenance on me as He healed my broken heart and carried away my pain!

It was so good to be in unity with God again, not just in my spirit but now unity within my whole being—spirit, soul, and body. I'm so glad God never compromises His calling for us because of our poor choices! His calling on us remains; what kind of God would stay and not abandon this new place of His grace? What kind of love is this? God never left this tabernacle, this temple, this life of mine. Our God's love is relentless and unexplainable!

God is really the first One who demonstrated an "extreme home makeover." He made all things new! Not only does He know how to build, but He knows how to restore and rebuild. "I will never leave you or forsake you" now has new meaning for me. He changed locations, for me! For you! He said He would build His church (we believers) and the gates of hell would not prevail against it (Matthew 16:18).

I am the place of His grace, and I'm part of something huge, new, and hated by the devil as the place of God's presence. I am all in, and there is nobody nowhere and nothing no how that could ever separate me from the love of God (Romans 8:39). I personally discovered that image really does produce identity—and who I worship and how I live matters!

Through learning that God will never leave me or forsake me, I now had a new determination that I would never again knowingly bow to a counterfeit image. I was created in God's image!

BOWING TO THE IMAGE

Genesis 1:27 tells us, *"So God created man in His own image, in the image of God He created him; male and female He created them."*

When God created physical beings as male and female, He created us in "His own image," which is obviously referring to spirit because God is Spirit. His own image is not a physical image—it is a spiritual image expressed in a physical body. God was never revealed in a physical body until the Word became flesh. The Word who always was became Jesus and was born both fully God and fully man. The Bible says that God is Spirit, so we were literally created as a spirit being in the image of God, making us eternal beings. We were created; we were made in the image of God Himself. Image is so powerful. Think about it!

What if we really believed the following Scripture passages?

For as he thinks in his heart, so is he (Proverbs 23:7).

As in water face reflects face, so a man's heart reveals the man (Proverbs 27:19).

*And as we have borne the image of the man of dust, we shall also **bear the image of the heavenly Man*** (1 Corinthians 15:49).

*For whom He foreknew, He also predestined to be conformed to **the image of His Son**, that He might be the firstborn among many brethren* (Romans 8:29).

*Therefore, if anyone is in Christ, he is a **new creation**; old things have passed away; behold, **all things have become new*** (2 Corinthians 5:17).

What Adam lost in the original creation, Jesus redeemed in the second creation. What Adam got wrong, Jesus got right. This is the reason Jesus is referred to as "the second Adam" in the book of Romans.

As my friend, Duane Sheriff, says in his powerful book *Identity Theft*, "There are two families in the world: Adam's family and God's family. You can choose to be a part of either one. Do you remember the old Addams Family television show? (The younger generation may have to Google it.) That was one messed-up family, but they thought everyone else was strange!"[2]

This is so funny but so true, isn't it? Little children think their family is "normal." They don't usually see the bigger picture until they begin to grow up. Reality may seem normal, but God's truth changes everything! God's family is forever!

God so loved the world that He sent His only Son so we could be family and take on His image and a new identity. The Word becoming flesh was vitally important. Jesus was the image of God in human form, and He came to show us the Father. God's original design was restored, revealed, and globally launched in Christ.

Image is a very important word to talk about and understand because it leads to identity. You will serve somebody, and your life is going to reflect what you value. Most people would not think image has anything to do with worship, but truthfully image has everything to do with worship! Let me show you what I mean by asking you: Who are you serving? Are you bowing to an image or bowing to *the* Image? Here is why it matters: *Image leads to identity and who we bow to is who will have authority in our lives.*

Worship is so much more than a song! It's so much more than what happens on a Sunday morning! Worship is a lifestyle, a way of life, and it's the giving of ourselves, submitting, and honoring God and responding to the One who loved us first. There are many biblical ways to express the heart of worship through outward expressions, but it's not about the expressions, the *how*, as much as it's about the *why*.

If you are a believer, a lover of God, then you are what the Bible calls a true worshiper. It's really that simple. Because of a New Covenant, you have a face-to-face relationship with God as Father, because God the Son and God the Holy Spirit take up residence in you. The Godhead helps you, leads you into truth, and shows you things to come. As a true worshiper, you contain His own image who is fully alive, thanks to Jesus who is Truth and Life and the *only* way to the Father. The image alive now in you produced a new identity, and now as a new creation you're living each day in what is known as the *believer's authority!* You've become a threat to the devil because you bowed your life to Jesus! Who you bow to is who you will serve. This is why worship and authority are linked.

You have an enemy who is out to steal, kill, and destroy you. He wants your life, your body, your very existence; if you won't give him any place in your life, he will still try to confuse, distort, and deceive you. He is the father of lies and would love to get you to doubt God's Word and instead believe a lie (John 8:44).

The enemy really wants you to bow your heart to someone else or something else; if you won't do that, at the very least he may fill up your life with stuff that just produces wood, hay, and stubble. A distorted image will make you feel pressed to stay busy all the time to feel needed and valued. Instead of making room for God in your day-to-day activities and blessing Him with all that is within you from a place of rest in knowing how loved and valued you are, eventually your heart will become overloaded. Then your heart will get hardened to the things of God, and eventually you will bow to another image instead of to *the* Image.

God wants us as believers to walk in the authority He gave us in Christ. The enemy is very aware of this and trying to steal from you what already belongs to you by getting you to bow to another image instead of the image of God.

Are you right now worried that a thief might steal $100,000 in cash that you have in your house? No, you probably aren't worried. Why? Because chances are you don't have $100,000 lying around your house, right? A thief can't steal what you don't have. So, because you have and are the image of God, the devil is the thief trying to steal that image from you.

Worship and the ground you give the enemy are incredibly connected and intimately linked. We will explore this idea more in-depth later, but because we have bowed our lives to Christ as believers we do have authority in the name of Jesus to live life supernaturally now, in this lifetime. The name of Jesus is *so* exalted that we need to see what Paul wrote about it in his letter to the Philippians:

> *Therefore God also has highly exalted Him and given Him the name which is above every name, that at the name of Jesus **every knee should bow,** of those in heaven, and of those on earth, and of those under the earth, and that every tongue should confess that Jesus Christ is Lord, to the glory of God the Father* (Philippians 2:9-11).

Even the devil knows the power of bowing your heart and how it is linked to authority. Bowing your knee is simply a physical expression of a bowed heart. Look at this:

> *Again, the devil took Him* [Jesus] *up on an exceedingly high mountain, and showed Him all the kingdoms of the world and their glory. And he said to Him, "All these things I will give You if You will **fall down and worship me"*** (Matthew 4:8-9).

What? Can you imagine trying to pull that stunt on Jesus? I mean, seriously. If the devil tried that on Jesus, you can rest assured that the devil doesn't want you to know whose image you've been created in naturally or recreated in spiritually. He really doesn't want you to know how loved you are by God, because once you know the truth, the truth will set you free to fully love God with your whole heart as a response to His love for you, therefore taking the authority that Jesus gave you to live life abundantly! The devil would love for you to be another case of stolen identity.

I think many people in the United States think that the worship of idols is something that happens in places like Africa, India, Indonesia, or some other country, but people worldwide still worship idols. And, dare I say, *especially* in America. We even have our own TV show called *American Idol!* I personally believe that Americans probably have even more idols than other countries, even though they might appear less obvious.

The enemy doesn't care which identity you have or how you identify yourself—as long as it's not in Christ.

Anything that takes God's place in your life is an idol. God prepared the table in the presence of your enemies; even the devil knows your provision, but he sure is trying to keep you from knowing it. So, who are you going to serve? To whom are you going to bow your heart? To whom are you going to yield yourself day by day?

> *Do you not know that to whom **you present your-selves** slaves to obey, you are that one's slaves whom you obey, whether of sin leading to death, or of obedience leading to righteousness?* (Romans 6:16)

*I beseech you therefore, brethren, by the mercies of God, that **you present your bodies** a living sacrifice, holy, acceptable to God, which is your reasonable service. And do not be conformed to this world, but be transformed by the renewing of your mind, that you may prove what is that good and acceptable and perfect will of God* (Romans 12:1-2).

WE WILL NEVER BOW DOWN

I want to take you back to the Old Covenant for a minute, where we can learn much from the life of Daniel. I personally identified with this story even as a very young man because of my name being Daniel, but there is something much more powerful in Daniel's "behind the scenes" life that should inspire and challenge everyone. This revelation of how Daniel lived couldn't be more relevant.

Daniel was from Jerusalem, probably from an upper-class family. When Jerusalem was besieged by Babylon, Daniel was a teenager who was taken captive to Shinar. He was required to be trained and educated for three years in the culture and language of his capturers, because King Nebuchadnezzar wanted him to know the ways of his kingdom so he could properly serve him. As the king of Babylon, he stole many of the articles from "the house of God" in Jerusalem and put them into the treasure house of his god in Babylon.

What a powerful picture of how jealous the enemy is over the treasure of God today—Christ in you! As the house of God, the temple of the Holy Spirit, you do know that you are the place of the treasure, right? Christ in you, the hope of glory has forever changed your image and your identity.

Daniel was physically perfect, good-looking, smart, gifted, and had favor all over him. But even though Daniel was a captive in their world, he refused to be of their world. He had a different image inside him, even from his childhood. Instead of being bitter, Daniel chose wisely to grow and learn and be better as a result. There was an image in him that led to an identity that he lived out loud.

Is it possible that Daniel still remembered the "house of God" in Jerusalem from his childhood? What do you think? Now, years later, as a teenager forced into captivity, is it possible that he was allowed to see into the treasure house of King Nebuchadnezzar, as he was being trained to serve him?

There was an image that Daniel brought with him from those early years that could not be trained out of him. The image he carried inside himself influenced how he lived his life, and that in turn influenced even his close Hebrew friends—and that was just the beginning. Every Hebrew boy knew the law and what the law of Moses had to say about image and worship:

> *And God spoke all these words, saying: "I am the Lord your God, who brought you out of the land of Egypt, out of the house of bondage. You shall have no other gods before Me. You shall not make for yourself a carved image—any likeness of anything that is in heaven above, or that is in the earth beneath, or that is in the water under the earth;* **you shall not bow down to them nor serve** [worship] **them.** *For I, the*

*Lord your God, am a jealous God, visiting the iniq-
uity of the fathers upon the children to the third and
fourth generations of those who hate Me, but showing mercy to thousands, to those who love Me and keep
My commandments* (Exodus 20:1-6).

In Daniel 3 we read how King Nebuchadnezzar made an
image. I want you to really get this in your mind's eye—he
made an image. It was an impressive image of his own invention, and even made of pure gold and about 90 feet tall by
9 feet wide. Huge! Even though it was a counterfeit image
and an image that was of human origin, can you imagine how
impressive it must have been to the people of Babylon? Wow!

The enemy still tries to overwhelm our hearts through
counterfeit images, trying to impress us through cheap imita-
tions. He hopes we will bow to his counterfeit image, resulting
in huge obstacles in our hearts against the known will of God.

For Daniel, even though the idol was impressive, he knew
it was an idol and contrary to God's design. Bowing to it would
be idolatry. The king and all the leadership of their country
made it illegal not to worship it—citizens had to worship the
idol. It was declared the law of the land, and with the sound of
"symphony with all kinds of music" the people were commanded
to bow to the image (Daniel 3:10).

Music can be powerfully used to impact a generation and
help establish an image. This enemy king of Israel knew that
submitting to this new image would eventually change the
identity of a generation!

When we, like Daniel, come to the place where we know what we believe and are not willing to compromise, we will refuse to bow our hearts and our lives to any other image of idolatry, whatever it is.

We need to submit to the Word of God, which results in the power of God working through us to bring change to the people around us—potentially even an entire nation. It's not that we are great, rather that God is great and greatly to be praised (1 Chronicles 16:25).

When we worship the created instead of the Creator, we bow to bondage and eventually connect with it as our identity.

What we believe we put into action, or we don't really believe it. God's Word is already alive and powerful, we just need to believe it! We never have to try to make the Word of God come true; it already is true! A lie doesn't become truth, wrong doesn't become right, and evil doesn't become good just because it's accepted by a majority!

Ecclesiastes 8:4 says, *"Where the word of a king is, there is power; and who may say to him, 'What are you doing?'"* The King of kings knows what He is doing. What He says is true!

Remember this—faith comes by hearing the Word of God, and when we believe God's report, denying the facts is not faith (Romans 10:17). The facts represent the reality we see, but faith is the evidence of things not seen (Hebrews 11:1).

Exalting the truth above the facts is faith—and only God's Word can change reality. Truth trumps reality!

In John 17:17 Jesus says, *"Sanctify them by Your truth. Your word is truth."*

It's foolish to try to redefine or change the Word of God. Okay, actually it's also really stupid! The entire Bible closes with a stern warning in Revelation 19:18-20 about adding or taking away from what God has said to be true. Don't go there! Really. You'll be there forever.

Dave Duell was my pastor in the late 1970s into 1981, and I had the blessing of serving on staff as his first worship leader. I also helped establish his first congregation from a college Bible study that started at the University of Northern Colorado in Greeley. He was an amazing man and had a profoundly positive impact on my life, including mentoring me in my early years of hearing the voice of God and doing life and ministry supernaturally. He just recently moved to heaven. Regarding salvation and eternity, he used to tell people, "It's only forever!" He would laugh at the power of this truth with a huge robust laugh, which I can still hear to this day, as if to say, "Trust me, I know what I'm talking about!"

Truth is always true! Even if you choose to not believe the truth, the truth remains the truth. Your doubt and unbelief don't change the truth.

Sadly, not everyone is going to heaven, contrary to popular opinion today; but everyone is going to live forever. Jesus said there was only one way to get there—through Him! He's not *a* way; *He is the only way!*

Jesus already paid for our sin, and gave us His righteousness in exchange, and told us not to choose death, but instead to choose life, abundant life. Eternal life in Christ Jesus. Only Jesus can give this kind of abundant life to us—and praise God, He has! (See John 10:10.) Our part is to believe it and receive it by faith!

Proverbs 14:34 says, *"Righteousness exalts a nation, but sin is a reproach to any people."*

God blessed Daniel to be a man who didn't live life on empty. He was a man of "excellent spirit, extraordinary, extreme, surpassing"—all words used to define the Hebrew word translated as "excellent." When God promoted Daniel to leadership as a governor, because of the spirit of excellence he had cultivated in his heart, the other leaders knew that the only way to find something against

> **What you believe about Jesus will transform you— and can change a whole nation!**

Daniel was to *"find it against him concerning the law of his God"* (Daniel 6:5).

When Daniel found out that the political or national leadership had made a law that was contrary to God's Word, he didn't picket, he didn't panic, he didn't riot—instead, he went home. I find this so interesting because as far as we know from Scripture, this was the first thing he did. He went home because he had already chosen something better—he knew his prayer closet was where he would be the most effective. He already had an image inside his heart that he was bowing to, no matter what!

What if on a national level Americans made focusing on our house more important than the White House? Whatever nation you're from, what if your national government was established on godly foundations? What if our homes weren't valued by the cost of our real estate but the cost of the ground of our heart? What if our focus on the family came from the revelation of God's Word instead of television or movies or what some legislators are asking us to embrace now as "the new normal"?

> **The image in Daniel's heart led to an identity that was expressed in authority!**

Are you bowing in worship to the Name above all names and expressing that authority in the face of legislation opposing godly activities? I believe it's time to take a stand with an excellent spirit that says, *"I will never bow down to anyone or anything but God!"*

Daniel did that; he took a stand and then went straight into his prayer closet, his chamber, to pray on his knees. In addition to praying and giving thanks before his God as was his custom, he opened his windows, right in the midst of adversity. This is huge! It was not only time to go in the closet but it was time to come out of the closet, the prayer closet, and take a stand! Actually, he didn't come out; he was called out, just like we are! (See Daniel 6:10-16.)

*But you are a chosen generation, a royal priesthood, a holy nation, His own special people, that you may proclaim the praises of Him who **called you out** of darkness into His marvelous light* (1 Peter 2:9).

Obviously, Daniel didn't care if those who were against him saw him. Daniel was going to do the will of God no matter what it cost him personally. Open up the windows!

Honestly, I have never found the will of God to be convenient *or* comfortable!

It is time for us to learn how to shut out the distractions and all the other voices telling us what we should be doing.

> **Daniel didn't change what he believed to please someone who didn't believe!**

They think their ideas are superior and exalting them above God and His Word is a better way to go; but God calls it "foolishness"! It's time to listen to God because that is what true worshipers do. It's time to listen and then whatever He says to you, just do it!

Daniel 4:37 says that *"those who walk in pride He is able to put down."*

Jesus says in Matthew 6:6, *"But you, when you pray, go into your room, and when you have shut your door, pray to your Father who is in the secret place; and your Father who sees in secret will reward you openly."*

And Jesus says, *"Whatever I tell you in the dark* [in the prayer closet or in private], *speak in the light; and what you hear in the ear, preach on the housetops"* (Matthew 10:27).

Daniel didn't believe God's Word out of convenience. He wasn't taking a stand because it was the popular thing to do. Daniel refused to bow to the law of the land because it was contrary to the Word of God. Daniel said he would not serve, would not bow, and would not worship a counterfeit image, no matter if it meant losing his own life. He wanted to live, but was willing to die for what he knew to be true.

Daniel knew what he believed and that it was the will of God. He did not *"frustrate the grace of God"* (Galatians 2:21 KJV), he trusted in God and defied the king's command (Daniel 3:28) to the point that he and his close friends yielded their bodies *"that they might not serve nor worship any god, except their own God"* (Daniel 3:28 KJV; check out Romans 12:1-2 again).

Because Daniel didn't bow, King Nebuchadnezzar did!

Whether you willingly bow now in worship or not, there will be a day when you will bow and confess that Jesus is Lord! Paul wrote, *"For it is written: 'As I live, says the Lord, every knee shall bow to Me, and every tongue shall confess to God'"* (Romans 14:11).

NOTES

1. Caroline M. Leaf, *Switch On Your Brain: The Key to Peak Happiness, Thinking, and Health* (Grand Rapids, MI: Baker Books, 2013).

2. Duane Sheriff, *Identity Theft* (Shippensburg, PA: Harrison House Publishers, 2017), 30.

2

THE WORSHIPER'S IMAGE

I believe that if my carnal or natural life becomes the place of my identification, it will be the place of my limitation as well.

> *How often they provoked Him in the wilderness, and grieved Him in the desert! Yes, again and again they tempted God, and limited the Holy One of Israel* (Psalm 78:40-41).
>
> *For with God nothing will be impossible* (Luke 1:37).
>
> *For in Him we live and move and have our being* (Acts 17:28).
>
> *Therefore, my brethren, you also have become dead to the law through the body of Christ, that you may be married to another—to Him who was raised from the dead, that we should bear fruit to God. For when we were in the flesh, the sinful passions which were aroused by the law were at work in our members to bear fruit to death. But now we have been delivered*

from the law, having died to what we were held by,
*so that **we should serve in the newness of the Spirit***
and not in the oldness of the letter (Romans 7:4-6).

As true worshipers, we have a relationship with God in Christ; in fact, we could say that spiritually speaking, *we are married to Christ* so that the fruit of the Spirit can be produced through us. We are married to the grace of God! We are supposed to be productive and serve in the newness of the Spirit—not the oldness of the Law. We are the body of Christ. We are the Church.

God never wanted us to be married to legalism! He wants us married to grace and to express grace in the earth; in other words, to be fruitful in the grace of God so that the very nature of God can find expression in how we live life. We would give place to this grace now in us so that grace can flow through us. God created life to happen through relationships. You can't live in the newness of the Spirit if you're living in the oldness of the letter. You cannot give what you do not have.

Being *married to grace* and expressing the *glory of His grace* in the earth today is for all believers.

Jesus paid the price we couldn't afford by giving His own life on our behalf so we could be forgiven and delivered from darkness. Through the grace of God found in Christ, we were bought with a price so we wouldn't have to be yoked to the law anymore. What incredible love! This incredible provision is available to all. As believers we are all married to Christ, spiritually speaking.

The devil wants us to identify with anyone or anything—except Christ—to keep us in a place of limitation; any god will do!

Ephesians 1:6 says that we are *"the praise of the glory of His grace."* The law has no glory for us today!

> *To them God willed to make known **what are the riches of the glory of this mystery** among the Gentiles: which is **Christ in you,** the hope of glory* (Colossians 1:27).

Christ in us is the mystery revealed! Until the time of the New Covenant and the dawn of the church, no one had a clue.

> *To me, who am less than the least of all the saints, this grace was given, that I should preach among the Gentiles the unsearchable riches of Christ, and to make all see what is **the fellowship of the mystery,** which from the beginning of the ages has been hidden in God who created all things through Jesus Christ; **to the intent that now the manifold wisdom of God might be made known by the church to the principalities and powers in the heavenly places*** (Ephesians 3:8-10).

The church, the body of Christ, is made up of individual people with Jesus as the Head of the body, and each of us as believers has a place in His grace. We are spiritually all members of His body; however, the great mystery of Christ and the church is reflected physically or tangibly through the institution of marriage in the two becoming one. It takes the seed of a man and the egg of a woman to produce a baby. There is no other way to be fruitful and multiply, naturally speaking.

So why would this natural image be connected to a spiritual image in the earth and why would the enemy be so bent on distorting, attacking, and trying to steal it if it weren't so valued in the heart of God—especially during this age of grace that we are living in called the church age, where the manifold wisdom of God is being manifest through the church, even to the devil.

Ephesians 5:30-32 says, *"For we are members of His body, of His flesh and of His bones. 'For this reason, a man shall leave his father and mother and be joined to his wife, and the two shall become one flesh.' This is a great mystery, but I speak concerning Christ and the church."*

The image of the worshiper is the image of the church.

As believers, we have a unique place in a spiritual family that is so intimate and yet so big that it's not only global but it's out of this world—literally, out of this world! The family is in heaven and earth!

The body of Christ covers the face of the earth and is expressed in families. This image of the partnership between Christ and the church, the "called out ones," is clearly being reflected through the natural or physical marriage relationship as well as spiritually, which is why we can't afford to accept a counterfeit identity. Generations will be profoundly influenced by our decisions and the resulting legacy.

God is Spirit, and there is only one way to have a relationship, which is Spirit to spirit. And there is only one way to worship, which is to worship in spirit and truth. To enter this relationship and receive this image of Christ and the church requires an identification with Christ, resulting in a "one spirit" relationship where the worshiper knows he or she is loved, and that union results in abundant life.

Ephesians 5 makes it very clear that as we live in a godly marriage and see that expression of two becoming "one flesh," it is the image of Christ loving the church and the church responding!

This image of the worshiper is under assault.

His will is for this image to be clearly seen in the marriage relationship between a man and a woman. The man, the husband, is the reflected image of Christ, and the wife is the reflected image of the church. That partnership is created for fruitfulness. God's plan, His will, has always been for us to bear much fruit, both naturally and spiritually.

We are supposed to see the marriage relationship expressed between a man and a woman, rooted in the love of God, and the fruit from that loving relationship as an expression of the image of God all around the world! What God has joined together we cannot afford to let humans mess up and put asunder!

*And I also say to you that you are Peter, and on this rock **I will build My church** [that's you], **and the gates of Hades shall not prevail against it**. And I* *will give you the keys of the kingdom of heaven, and whatever you bind on earth will be bound in heaven, and whatever you loose on earth will be loosed in heaven* (Matthew 16:18-19).

*And He is before all things, and in Him all things consist. And **He is the head of the body, the church,** who is the beginning, the firstborn from the dead, that in all things He may have the preeminence* (Colossians 1:17-18).

*And He put all things under His feet, and gave Him to be head over all things to **the church, which is His body**, the fullness of Him who fills all in all* (Ephesians 1:22-23).

*And as we have borne the **image** of the man of dust, we shall also bear the **image** of the heavenly Man* (1 Corinthians 15:49).

In Chapter 1, the reason I shared the biblical account of Daniel refusing to bow to a counterfeit image or a substitute image—an image of idolatry—is to show how relevant it is right now in our generation and why it matters. We need to learn from this. Please don't miss this and think that worship is about a song.

As worshipers of God we have to choose who we are going to bow to. We will be challenged to bow to all kinds of man-made images, ideas, and laws that oppose the image of God, the image of the new creation, and all that is contained in the Word of God. What's true? Who's speaking the truth in love? How can we know for sure?

> *For this reason* **I bow my knees to the Father of our Lord Jesus Christ**, *from whom the whole family in heaven and earth is named* (Ephesians 3:14-15).

We have to decide who we are going to bow to and prepare our hearts ahead of time! Anytime you are being asked to conform to something that is contrary to the Word of God, you are being asked to bow. Let me show you what I mean and why this pertains to worship.

One of the big news topics in 2015 was that the Supreme Court of the United States declared that "same sex marriage" was now legal. This came to the surface of our national consciousness as a debate here in the United States about "civil unions" and personal rights centered on "same sex sexuality." This quickly evolved into a legal battle about the word "marriage."

There is so much I could say about marriage after years of doing marriage counseling, but this book is about worship, which is rooted in image and an identity and your authority. This is about relationship!

The word "marriage" biblically is used to define holy matrimony between a man and a woman, and God created it—we didn't. The Bible has much to say about relationships and how to live a prosperous, meaningful life; however, some of the leadership of this country have redefined the word "marriage" to now be mandated into law to also include "same sex marriage" as "marriage."

Isn't it interesting and obvious, however, that the words "same sex" must be included in the redefining of marriage to make it different? God clearly already created the image and identity for a fruitful marriage, defining that it is between a man and a woman long before government even existed. The institution of marriage goes all the way back to Genesis.

Once again, like in Daniel's day, government is changing the image, setting it up, and commanding us to accept it. Because it is now the law of the land, we're being told that we need to bow down to it, even with the sound of *all kinds of music in symphony*" to help us bow. Really?!

There is a powerful agenda happening right now to change the image of Christ and the church—as seen in a godly marriage between a man and a woman—into a sexual identity instead. God's Word has much to say about marriage—what it is and what it isn't. It is an image that leads to an identity, and without a godly revelation about this, sadly, we will accept a cheap imitation with no glory in it at all!

> **I have never referred to my marriage as an "opposite sex marriage," have you?**

Marriage is being redefined by the courts, by judges, and through the influence of people who have exalted their opinions above the Word of God, which is never a good idea, ever! How does a same-sex marriage produce children? It doesn't take a degree in science to figure out that being fruitful and multiplying doesn't happen between two women or two men. How is the glory of God going to cover the earth like the waters cover the sea without people? He can't be "Christ in us" without us! God created us male and female and called us *very good!*

Coming up with what you think is a better idea didn't work for Nebuchadnezzar, and it won't work well for anyone else either. Many leaders over the years who thought their opinions concerning an image were greater than the image of God discovered how futile it is to oppose the original Designer and Creator of all.

I'm going to show you how the redefining of marriage is about a strategy bigger than sexual identity or personal preference, and here it is—*redefining marriage is about worship.* This issue of marriage being redefined and the resulting image has to do with worship at its core, which is why I am passionate that you know your identity in Christ and refuse to live with a stolen identity.

In John 4:23-24 Jesus says, *"But the hour is coming, and now is, when the true worshipers will worship the Father in spirit and truth; for the Father is seeking such to worship Him. God is Spirit, and those who worship Him must worship in spirit and truth."*

We will talk more about this in the next chapter, but let me point out that *God is not looking for worship.* He is, however, looking for believers who are true worshipers. God is looking for relationship. He is looking for you! He knows if He has you, if He has your heart, worship will flow in spirit and truth.

Even unbelievers worship, they just don't worship the true God; they worship a false image, including each other. We all worship! Think for a minute what you used to worship instead of God. What were you bowing your heart to?

What is the opposite of worship in spirit and truth? Worship in flesh and lie? That even sounds stupid, doesn't it? Don't allow yourself to be ripped off.

> *Beware lest anyone cheat you through philosophy and empty deceit, according to the tradition of men, according to the basic principles of the world, and not according to Christ* (Colossians 2:8).

It is clear to me that the spirit of antichrist is at work right now setting up another image, a contrary image, a substitute image, for us to bow to today just like in Daniel's generation. By altering and modifying the image of Christ and the church into something without glory and something powerless to reproduce, the result is a stolen identity, having form and no power! The enemy is a thief and the author of confusion. He is the accuser of believers and committed to destroying the biblical image of marriage.

Whenever we exchange truth for a lie, we also change the object of our worship from the Creator to the created!

The devil wants to change the image of Christ and the church into his own perverted image of worshipers worshiping him and each other instead of God our Father. It's amazing how many churches are now being founded on "sexual identity" instead of identity in Christ. There are even churches now that come together as atheists. Talk about an oxymoron! The very word "church" means "called out ones."

> *For the wrath of God is revealed from heaven against all ungodliness and unrighteousness of men, who suppress the truth in unrighteousness, because what may be known of God is manifest in them, for God has shown it to them. For since the creation of the world His invisible attributes are clearly seen, being understood by the things that are made, even His eternal power and Godhead, so that they are without excuse, because, although they knew God, they did not glorify Him as God, nor were thankful, but became futile in their thoughts, and their foolish hearts were darkened. Professing to be wise, they became fools,* **and changed the glory of the incorruptible God into an image** *made like corruptible man—and birds and four-footed animals and creeping things.*
>
> *Therefore God also gave them up to uncleanness in the lusts of their hearts, to dishonor their bodies among themselves,* **who exchanged the truth of God for the lie, and worshiped and served the creature rather than the Creator,** *who is blessed forever. Amen.*
>
> *For this reason God gave them up to vile passion. For even their women exchanged the natural use for what is against nature. Likewise also the men leaving the natural use of the woman, burned in their lust for one another, men with men committing what*

is shameful, and receiving in themselves the penalty of their error which was due. And even as they did not like to retain God in their knowledge, God gave them over to a debased mind, to do those things which are not fitting (Romans 1:18-28).

Who are you bowing to? Culture or Christ? Don't let the "oldness of the letter" or "the vain traditions of men" define your image or your identity. What's in God's heart? What does His Word say?

DISTORTING THE IMAGE

I'll never forget the first time I saw my reflection in those trick mirrors at a county fair when I was a kid. Did you ever do that? Remember the one that made you look short and fat, and then the one that made you look super tall and thin, which humorously always seemed to be the more preferred mirror by most people. But, preferred or not, each mirror still reflected a distorted image.

Many times in Scripture, we see the enemy lying and using deception to counter and distort the image of God. Whose image is being reflected when we look in the mirror—self or the image of God?

One time in particular, the devil stooped to an all-time low when he persuaded the people to make an idol image using the very gold that God had blessed His people with when they left Egypt. This story is told in Exodus 32. That gold was their provision. Yet God, knowing they would end up misusing it, still gave it to them. Think about that for a while! God had an image of blessing for them in His heart, and instead of seeking Him they sold out for a cheap imitation—but God still didn't withhold His part.

When the people were under pressure, they defaulted to what was familiar. Their identity was at risk! They took the gold that God gave them and made a copy of an Egyptian god in the form of a golden calf. They distorted the image and bowed down to it, substituting God's Word with a graven image (Exodus 20:4). They clearly knew they were to have no other gods before Almighty God.

Pressure will always expose what's inside, revealing the heart.

Psalm 106:19-20 says, *"They made a calf in Horeb, and worshiped the molded image. Thus they changed their glory into the image of an ox that eats grass."*

Because they worshiped a molded image of a calf, they changed (exchanged) their God-given glory into the image of an ox. Instead of worshiping the Creator, they worshiped the created.

If they would have repented of this sin of idolatry, their lives would have been spared; but instead, when the golden calf was destroyed, they were destroyed as well because they had taken the image of the golden calf into their soul. The image was already inside their minds, and they were opposing themselves! When we substitute humanistic ideas for God's Word, we create an idol, which takes His place in our lives—and it is *always* a bad decision.

And we know that the Son of God has come and has given us an understanding, that we may know Him *who is true; and we are in Him who is true, in His Son Jesus Christ. This is the true God and eternal life. Little children, **keep yourselves from idols**. Amen* (1 John 5:20-21).

The devil doesn't really care what image we worship as long as it is an image other than the one true God. It's mind boggling to me how people can worship anyone or anything and be considered open-minded and forward thinkers. Yet when people are true worshipers of the Lord Jesus Christ, they are considered narrow-minded and backward thinkers. It is tragic, but we know where it's coming from—the devil. Another image, another idol, another substitute, another gospel = deception!

Let me ask you something. When people swear and use curse words, why don't they use the name of Mohammed or Confucius "in vain"? Why not Buddha or some other so-called god? There is only one true God; even the demons believe that and tremble according to James 2:19 (at least *they* tremble)! There have been many great leaders down through history, but when they are exalted to a god status, that is ignorance. The apostle Paul addressed this issue when writing to the church in Corinth:

I do not want you to be ignorant: You know that you were Gentiles, carried away to these dumb idols, however you were led (1 Corinthians 12:1-2).

And what agreement has the temple of God with idols? For you are the temple of the living God. As God has said: "I will dwell in them and walk among them. I will be their God, and they shall be My people" (2 Corinthians 6:16).

Do not be unequally yoked together with unbelievers.
For what fellowship has righteousness with lawless-
ness? And what communion has light with darkness?
(2 Corinthians 6:14)

God is so creative and so amazing that even nature itself shows and tells us about Him. His life is reflected everywhere. But we've been called to worship Him—not something else or ourselves or each other. We must not exchange His truth, which is always His Word, for a lie or what seems to be a better idea of our own invention.

In John 17:17, Jesus was praying to His Father and said, *"Sanctify them* [set them apart] *by Your truth. Your word is truth."*

Again, truth will always trump your reality if you allow it, even if your reality is a broken image. Truth in love will always cause you to stand out and stand up!

The enemy of God is after your worship. He even appears as an angel of light when necessary to accomplish his deception. He wants God's original image and design to be distorted and eventually destroyed. Again, remember, he even tried to get Jesus to bow down and worship him. Can you imagine? Satan is so envious of our relationship and our intimacy with God that his obsession will eventually lead to a human being, a man, who will yield to this evil spirit, an image he will identify with, and will allow himself to literally be possessed by it—and he will become the antichrist.

God's word tells us, *"The man of sin is revealed, the son of perdition, who opposes and exalts himself above all that is called God or that is worshiped, so that he sits as God in the temple of God, showing himself that he is God"* (2 Thessalonians 2:3-4). Can you see that he is self-absorbed? Self-centered?

It's always about worship, isn't it? It still is about worship! The devil wants to destroy your temple by messing up your identity in Christ. You do know you are the temple, right?

CHANGE THE IMAGE, CHANGE THE IDENTITY, CHANGE THE OUTCOME

The devil wants us to worship him instead of Jesus. He would love Christ Jesus to be replaced with an empty form and no power. His plan is to pervert the image of Christ in us, the church, and be our accuser in the church so that we will change the image and then pervert and swap the identity. Instead of seeing Christ and the church, the world at that point would see envy and strife and every evil work. Just like a bad marriage, he would love to see us tolerated rather than celebrated.

This will seem silly at first when you read it, but think about this—when people don't believe the truth, they believe a lie! They are willing to believe a lie because they wouldn't believe the truth. If you won't believe the truth, you will believe a lie!

We do this all the time with things like healing, for instance. Many won't believe the truth that healing was already provided for us in Christ, because we'd rather believe the reality of our physical symptoms of sickness and disease to be greater.

Any time we exalt our ideas above the Word of God, we create a counterfeit and ultimately an idol. What we exalt creates an image in our hearts that influences how we think and then how we live. We often live a lifetime in a broken image instead of the image of God! Not too different from Adam and Eve in the book of Genesis, many in the world today, thinking they are being "tolerant" or "open minded" to a different way of living, are substituting their plan in place of God's plan. Many think, *Did God say...? Is that really what He meant? Come on, that may be the ideal, but we live in the real world.*

Our enemy is so obsessed with being exalted and worshiped that he even tried to get Jesus to bow down and worship him three times! He still wants to destroy the image of God in the earth today, whether he is trying to destroy your temple, your body, or the image of the body of Christ, because that's who he is—the destroyer! The devil wants so desperately to destroy the idea of humans being made in God's image, hoping most people will never discover the image of Christ living in them through the second birth and the hope of glory, resulting in power to be witnesses!

Because the presence of God lives in us today by the indwelling Spirit of God, then wouldn't it make sense if you are the enemy of God to discredit that idea or, at the very least, try to change it into something else? The enemy logically tries to create a counterfeit or a substitute of some kind. If you were the enemy, wouldn't it make total sense to try to destroy the very idea of the "mystery of Christ in us"—us being the church, the body of Christ, or the place of His presence today?

I hope by now that I have painted a clear picture of the enemy's agenda and how he uses people to accomplish it. He uses things like redefining marriage and the destructive patterns of sexual brokenness against us, but he also has many other devices including sickness, debt, stress, our own lack of knowledge about how he works, and years of wrong teaching in the church, just to name a few. As a deceiver, a liar, he tries to destroy the image of God in the earth and comes to steal our true identity in Christ. He even uses portions of the Word against us to stop us from becoming true worshipers.

Let me give you a completely different example of what I mean. Many believers are coming together, which is good, but they are coming together week after week asking God to show up—and that's not good! How can they as believers not know that the Holy Spirit of God is already in them? Talk about messed up! He is the "I Am" and the "Always Present One." He's not the Great I Was or the Great I Used To Be. He changed location just to be *in us;* not knowing that results in

Many in the church are living under the wrong covenant and don't even know it.

not participating. You won't engage and partner with the Spirit of God in the earth today if you don't even know He's alive and powerful in you, right now.

Why would people think they have to ask Him to show up as if He is a "no show" or an absent God, missing in action, somewhere out there. Through ignorance the Bible says we perish. This is so true! Through ignorance and unbelief, much of the church is not being fruitful today as a result.

The enemy wants us to be blind to what God has done and what He has given us. He thinks of ways to discredit and dishonor us. He is working overtime to change the image. If he can get us to think that Christ is "going to do" something, we will always come up short. Aren't you tired of every January being the year of "_____"? Fill in the blank. Every year, something is promised that is "going to happen" that Jesus already provided for us and already did for us. I know there are seasons and things that the Holy Spirit will emphasize, but when it comes to what Jesus already did for us, it is a done deal, friend!

Some believers think that even though every promise is yes and amen, these same New Covenant promises are "not yet" or are "time-released" promises.

As believers, we are the church and the body of Christ in the earth today, and we get to cooperate with Jesus, the Head of the church, and do what He is doing and say what He is saying. We are the location of His presence on earth. The Holy Spirit is only going to confirm what Jesus has already done. He will lead us into all truth, but not because He somehow has to add more truth to what is already there. He always confirms the Word of God and He does it through us!

We are His voice in the earth today. We need to speak the Word, and speak it boldly! Speak it to the mountains in your life and watch them move. It's time to start shouting "Grace" to some high places and some hard things that the enemy has exalted. Speak to the mountains on behalf of others in need of breakthrough.

LET NO ONE SEPARATE

God has joined us together with Himself so that right now we can partner in the earth and nothing can separate us from Him or His love for us. In Matthew 19:6, Jesus Himself answered their question with this answer, *"Therefore what God has joined together, let no one separate"* (NRSV).

This phrase "let no one separate" is so foundational to the adventure of being a worshiper in our generation and learning to live a lifestyle of worship! What God joined together, we must not let anyone redefine or separate from God's truth. God joined us together with Him through Jesus! We are not married to the Old Covenant law.

> **We have a better covenant with better promises and a better way to worship!**

Worship from the inside out as Christ followers is New Covenant worship and it is so much better than Old Covenant worship! The Old Covenant was outside in, while the New Covenant is always inside out. Worship from the inside out is our new normal.

> But now He has obtained a more excellent ministry, inasmuch as **He is also Mediator of a better covenant,** which was established on better promises (Hebrews 8:6).
>
> For **in Him** we live and move and have our being (Acts 17:28).

Jesus came from heaven to earth to pay our price for sin by becoming sin who knew no sin. He took on our sickness, brokenness, and shame and fully finished what needed to be done to show us the image of the heavenly Father—then He returned to heaven with us in His heart! We were the joy that was set before Him, and we still are! His manifest love changed our location from death to life and from legalism to grace!

Romans 8:38-39 says, *"For I am persuaded that neither death nor life, nor angels nor principalities nor powers, nor things present nor things to come, nor height nor depth, nor any other created thing, shall be able to separate us from the love of God which is in Christ Jesus our Lord."*

This picture of marriage and Christ and the church is for *now*—for our generation. It is for this time that we are living in because once we are in heaven there is no more marriage. Once we are in heaven, there will no longer need to be a representation, because we will be living in the full manifestation!

> *For in the resurrection they neither marry nor are given in marriage, but are like angels of God in heaven* (Matthew 22:30).
>
> *Let us be glad and rejoice and give Him glory, for the marriage of the Lamb has come, and His wife has made herself ready* (Revelation 19:7).

Speaking of marriage…

3

DIVINE APPOINTMENTS DEFY SOCIAL BARRIERS

In one of the most amazing Bible stories, Jesus shows us how the presence of God is expressed in relationship and what Jesus says concerning this truth of a coming location change. He spoke to a woman at a well who, much like me at one time in my life, was living in sin and trying to fit in. Do you still remember those days in your own life?

We don't even know her name, but here in this place of thirst Jesus gave what I consider to be the greatest revelation of worship in the entire Bible. It is such a beautiful picture of grace and a powerful lesson of God's unconditional love, and what can still happen when we live from a redeemed identity in Christ.

In the Gospel of John chapter 4 we find the very famil-iar story of the woman at the well. It is so familiar to most

Christians that we may tune it out when being preached. I know, because I grew up in church hearing this story so many times that I wasn't listening anymore like I should have been.

Several years ago, I was fasting and praying and spending time in this passage of Scripture and it was as if I started seeing it with new eyes and hearing it with new ears! I even wondered if my version of the Bible had been changed somehow. It had such impact on my heart that it even changed my ministry!

Divine appointments often defy social barriers.

Jesus left Judea on a 37-mile journey to Galilee. John 4:4 says, *"He needed to go through Samaria."* I believe God had a divine appointment scheduled at that ancient well, a place of public shame and emotional pain for a Samaritan woman; her past had followed her into her present. Little did she know that she was the reason that Jesus needed to go through Samaria. Just like we are the reason Jesus *needed to go* to the cross and through hell on our behalf.

> So He came to a city of Samaria which is called
> Sychar, near the plot of ground that Jacob gave to his
> son Joseph. Now Jacob's well was there. Jesus therefore,
> being wearied from His journey, sat thus by the well.
> It was about the sixth hour [noon] (John 4:5-6).

Jesus was physically tired, showing us that He was indeed 100 percent human, even though He was 100 percent God. After walking 37 miles we would be tired, too. God was about to demonstrate His love to the "least of these" (Matthew

25:40,45). The woman's empty pots and empty life were about to be filled with living water.

> *A woman of Samaria came to draw water. Jesus said to her, "Give Me a drink." For His disciples had gone away into the city to buy food. Then the woman of Samaria said to Him, "How is it that You, being a Jew, ask a drink from me, a Samaritan woman?" For Jews have no dealings with Samaritans* (John 4:7-9).

It is amazing to see how the grace of God will lead us into divine appointments that defy social barriers. I believe we often miss the supernatural in the everyday while looking for the spectacular. If we trust Him and just do the natural, God will do the supernatural through us. God loves appointments with the lost one—not just the ninety-nine who are found. He loves people! He loves the weak, the despised, the foolish, and what seem to be the insignificant, even the rejected. And He loves demonstrating His love and His grace through you and me to everyone. We are the place of His dwelling, so why wouldn't He?

What was going on in Sychar isn't really that different from what is going on in your city or any city or culture today. Some people groups seem to be so against one another, and sometimes it overflows into full on war with nation against nation. The Jews and the Samaritans were historic enemies.

> *Jesus answered and said to her, "If you knew the gift of God, and who it is who says to you, 'Give Me a drink,' you would have asked Him, and He would have given you **living water**." The woman said to*

*Him, "Sir, You have nothing to draw with, and the well is deep. Where then do You get that living water? Are You greater than our father Jacob, who gave us the well, and drank from it himself, as well as his sons and his livestock?" Jesus answered and said to her, "Whoever drinks of this water will thirst again, but whoever drinks of the water that I shall give him will never thirst. But **the water that I shall give** him will become in him **a fountain of water springing up into everlasting life**." The woman said to Him, "Sir, give me this water, that I may not thirst, nor come here to draw"* (John 4:10-15).

Jesus is telling the woman about "living water" and how the living water would be in her and what was in her would spring up into everlasting life. John 6:63 says, *"It is the Spirit who gives life; the flesh profits nothing. The words that I speak to you are Spirit, and they are life."* And then we discover this in John 7:37-39:

*On the last day, that great day of the feast, Jesus stood and cried out, saying, **"If anyone thirsts, let him come to Me and drink**. He who believes in Me, as the Scripture has said, **out of his heart will flow rivers of living water**." But this He spoke concerning the Spirit, whom those believing in Him would receive; **for the Holy Spirit was not yet given, because Jesus was not yet glorified**.*

What a huge, important statement! The Holy Spirit was not yet given, because Jesus was not yet glorified. We will deal with His glorification in more detail later.

When Jesus came, He was the child who was born and the Son who was given. The Word of God became a human being born of a woman, but that woman was not impregnated by a man—rather, supernaturally by the Holy Spirit. Jesus was born by the Spirit of God. The Word that had always been became flesh!

Under the Old Covenant, many experienced the Spirit of God coming upon them for a specific assignment that God wanted them to carry out, but they didn't have the Spirit of God living in them. When the Word became flesh, He was given the name Jesus, and because He was born into an Old Covenant system He also needed to have the Spirit of God come upon Him for His earthly ministry because of the limitations of a physical body, just like so many did before Him under the Old Covenant.

Aren't you glad that He came to fulfill the Old Covenant system so the Spirit of God could be given! No one else had the Spirit of God living in them yet. The Spirit of God was not given to live inside people until after the redemption of humankind through the cross and the resurrection of Jesus.

WHEN WAS THE SPIRIT OF GOD GIVEN?

The Spirit of God was given to people after Jesus returned to heaven to be seated at the right hand of the Father. This is when the Spirit of God could be given—not a minute before!

This gift is so huge—Jesus was giving us a new image of what was coming. We now know this is the time of establishing the church, the body of Christ on earth.

The price for us to be the church was paid for on the cross, and when His side was opened the veil of the old system was torn in two from top to bottom. God removed the bride of Christ from His side, very much like when He brought Eve to Adam. That was physical, and this was spiritual. When Jesus died on the cross and rose to His rightful seat beside His heavenly Father, His children on earth became new creations from the inside out for the first time in history!

No one really had a clue what the church was in Jesus' day. Many today have the opposite problem; we have become so familiar with the idea of church that we have lost the power of the revelation and think it's a place to go to in order to worship God. The Holy Spirit was about to move into humanity for the first time in history and turn our bodies into temples. We were about to become the place where worship would happen.

This Gospel period was a transitional time that eventually brought an end to the Old Covenant when Jesus was crucified, rose from the dead, and ascended into heaven. Only then could the Holy Spirit come and remain here; only then could the Holy Spirit of God be given. Think about it—Jesus had to physically leave in order for the Holy Spirit to remain here.

Jesus was the beginning of the New Covenant. We really have no idea how blessed we are to have the very Spirit of God living in us, and yet so many people don't even know He is here. They think it's up to them to do something to get the Holy Spirit to come. Really? Think about how crazy that really is. It's as if what God planned from the foundation of the world isn't enough. It's a counterfeit image to think that way, isn't it?

In the John 4 passage, Jesus shows a new, true image to the woman at the well. Jesus is showing His love to an "enemy of Israel" and giving her so much more than she realized—and more than most of us have yet to realize.

Jesus is dealing with this woman's heart and speaking of Himself as the Gift of God and Living Water. Jesus met her where she was. His passion for knowing the heart of His Father was spilling out into compassion for hers. This divine appointment that defied social barriers was going to spring up into everlasting life at some point soon, even though she didn't know it yet. The supernatural often happens in the midst of the natural. The supernatural presence of God is always expressed in relationship.

Jesus said that once the life of God moves inside of your spirit, you never thirst again, and that spiritual thirst is satisfied forever! God never intended His life to just be life upon us or even just life within us! It was always His plan that what was in our spirit would spring up into our soul and throughout our body—and the life of Christ within would not only be a blessing to us but also become someone's miracle, someone's blessing as it flows out from us!

God always deals with us on a heart level, and Jesus showed us how to do it. This divine appointment beside an ancient well became a demonstration of the love of God that brought refreshment and life.

Jesus said to her, "Go, call your husband, and come here." The woman answered and said, "I have no husband." Jesus said to her, "You have well said, 'I have no husband,' for you have had five husbands, and the one whom you now have is not your husband; in that you spoke truly" (John 4:16-18).

Jesus not only saw her empty water pots, but He saw the emptiness in her heart by the Spirit of God. Jesus heard a word that was given to Him just for her. Cooperating with the Spirit, beyond what was being said by her spoken words, He went for her heart! Even though her heart was broken and still trying to find someone to quench her thirst for love, Jesus saw past the physical and went right into "the well of her heart" of what was really going on to help this woman see a reflection of more than herself.

He was not intimidated by her brokenness, nor is He by yours. When we recognize our need for a Savior, we experience unconditional love that opens us up to a brand-new beginning and a brand-new life. God has divine appointments waiting for you that defy social barriers. Are you ready? Are you willing?

Sexual brokenness in any manner is not anything new to God. Remember though, even now in our generation where sin abounds, grace abounds much more! I believe the enemy thinks he has scored a huge victory in redefining marriage and trying to destroy the image of Christ and the church that a Christian marriage covenant represents. He wants us to believe marriage can be between anyone or anything, as we discussed in the last chapter. Even though the enemy thinks he has won this, I can tell you without hesitation that God is greater!

But think about this. Why would God give the greatest revelation of a Spirit-to-spirit, face-to-face relationship called true worship to a messed-up woman who was obviously not doing well at marriage and still living in adultery? She was a sexually broken person who had had five husbands, and the one she was with was not her own. Now, Jesus, You're going to give this revelation about being a true worshiper of God to her...really?

Remember, Jesus only says what His Father gives Him to say (John 12:49).

God knew this revelation was going to be foundational in establishing the image and identity of Christ and the church as reflected in marriage. Jesus knew who this woman at the well was. Weren't there more important people to give this revelation to, this revelation that would be foundational in the church for centuries to come?

Jesus only did what the Father told Him to do, and I believe it was all on purpose and for a higher purpose. Jesus came to heal the brokenhearted and God wanted us to know that no one is too far gone or messed up. No one is too hard-hearted or too impossible for His love to open up their hearts so He can speak truth. He wanted us to see the grace of God in action through the love and truth Jesus gave to the woman and what happened as a result. I believe it was very intentional. It was, indeed, a divine appointment defying social barriers. This amazing grace is foundational for a true worshiper.

MESSY PLACES

God wanted to show us a very clear picture that messy places aren't a problem for Him, not only in the way He ministered to this woman at the well but even in the way He sent Jesus to the earth. I mean, if you were God Almighty and you were sending the King of kings and the Lord of lords who was the Word about to be made flesh, it would only make sense that you would send Him in the finest of heaven's royal garb and into the finest palace. Instead, God made a statement by allowing Jesus to be born in a manger. A manger, yes, a messy place where animals were fed—literally a feeding trough. This is where Jesus lay as a newborn baby. I grew up in rural North Dakota and Montana, so ask me how I know that where animals feed, they also mess!

One Christmas not long ago, as I was watching *The Nativity,* one of my favorite Christmas movies, I wondered why God introduced Jesus into the world in this way. During this particular viewing of the movie, I was ministered to by the Holy Spirit as He showed me why Jesus was born in a manger. I felt God wanted us to know that He is not afraid of our messy places, our messy lives, or our messy circumstances—so He made sure Jesus was born in one! He came to where we are!

He eventually took to the cross all the sin and all the mess and literally became sin for us even though He never personally sinned. He took our sin, our mess, our brokenness, our sickness and disease and pain and gave us His life in exchange. What a deal!

It's significant that Jesus gave this living water revelation to the nameless woman at the well and communicated the love of the Father, helping her to experience the very presence of God. This woman is similar to another unnamed woman in Scripture. She is known only as "the adulterous woman" to whom Jesus ministered in another supernatural divine appointment that defied social barriers. She was delivered of seven demons—imagine that for a minute. She then later, as a thank you and an act of worship, broke her bottle of super-expensive perfume that cost a year's salary and poured it on Jesus' head, and the fragrance filled the room.

What really filled the room that night was the fragrance of her thanksgiving for Jesus giving her a new life. Her testimony is now told wherever the gospel is preached. Her mess became her message, and ours too! The good news of the gospel goes beyond any social barrier!

What do we take away from seeing Jesus minister to the poor and sick; touching the untouchable, the hurting, and the brokenhearted; as well as the powerful, rich, and famous? How did Jesus minister the presence of God to people from every walk of life? The Father wanted us to clearly see who God really is by seeing Jesus doing what He did in love and compassion.

When the supernatural life of God flows, transformation does too!

Now, let's return to John 4 to read how the woman at the well responded to Jesus ministering to her as He spoke directly to her situation. He listened to what the Father was saying, and said that to her. *"The woman said to Him, 'Sir, I perceive that You are a prophet'"* (John 4:19). I bet she did! I mean, here is a Man who "reads her mail," spiritually speaking, so of course she thought He was a prophet. This brief sentence went right by me for years; now, here's why I think it's even more significant.

The Samaritans didn't accept any of the writings of the prophets as inspired Scripture because Samaria was prophetically and publicly denounced many times by the prophets God sent to them, primarily because of their worship of Baal. Baal was a god of fertility, and worship included witchcraft and sacrificing babies as well as making their sons and daughters walk through fire in their pagan rituals. Any god other than the one true God leads to a dead end. Literally!

Actually it was very similar to Israel—when God sent a prophet to them, instead of repenting, the Samaritans typically hardened their hearts and brought in more religions with more gods.

Isn't it interesting how once we reject the truth we are then willing to believe a lie? We always have a choice to either turn around and obey God's Word or not. If we're going to reject the truth, then another option would be to just take out the prophets because they aren't saying what we want them to say, right? That's just what they did.

They had their own Samaritan version of Scripture, which back then was the Law and the five books of Moses. The books of the prophets were Jewish prophets, so the Samaritans didn't believe in the prophets. Most Samaritans believed the Jewish prophets were always prophesying about getting rid of their foreign idols and their resulting sin of idolatry, which was true, but certainly not the whole story.

When we open ourselves to idolatry and bow to any idol in any generation, we end up in some kind of captivity in our hearts, which limits how we live our lives. Remember, idols are always a dumb idea!

Because of their sin, the Samaritans were conquered; and because they ignored God's messengers and even killed them in brutal ways, they proved they didn't want to hear the Word of the Lord even though God kept warning them. The result was disaster and physical destruction; even worse, the enemies brought new images for them to worship, including Baal.

Samaria was not the only nation impacted by idolatry. Israel was also impacted through the worship of Baal. Satan knew if he could change their image, he could change their identity. I find this process of Baal worship and the name Baal very significant. Not only was it the name of the idol but also one of the Hebrew words for "husband." God wanted to be the people's Husband, so the enemy counterfeited once again something God designed for good! The enemy's tactic was to change the image to change the identity. That remains his tactic today—gay no longer means happy, and the rainbow no longer represents a promise from God but a symbol of a sexual revolution.

Even though the Jews and the Samaritans had no dealings with each other, it is interesting they were all dealing with the same issues of the heart.

When Jesus said to this Samaritan woman, "Go, call your husband, and come here," something life-changing started happening in her heart. He brought the very presence of God to where she was living.

Women didn't usually go to the well at noon to draw water if their identity was intact. They went in the early morning when it was cooler and connected with other women who would be there at that time of day as well. That was common practice during this generation.

But this unnamed woman had a broken identity; she had probably been wounded and abused multiple times in her life. Because her image of herself was so distorted, she saw very little value in herself, but God had a divine appointment waiting that would defy social barriers and break through the broken image that was in her heart. Other people looked at the outward appearance and saw "damaged goods," but Jesus saw her heart, value, and worth, as He always does!

Jesus was showing us how to live grace out loud and establish a culture of grace. The gospel was never intended to be only a teaching. God used Jesus, His Word, to reveal the heart of the circumstances. All the broken pieces of her life finally seemed to connect, and she felt like she had found the One she was longing for, and she said to Him, *"Sir, I perceive that You are a prophet."*

The Lord, knowing she was looking for a soul mate, someone who would complete her, knew how frustrated she had been. Any time we look to another person to complete us, spiritually speaking, is idolatry, which always leads to frustration. No human on earth can meet the unrealistic expectation of being someone else's purpose. Jesus is the only One who can fill that place. He is the only One who could make the woman a brand-new creation.

Jesus not only met her while she filled her pots, but He met her where she was and filled her life.

Notice what He doesn't do. He doesn't condemn her. He doesn't point out her sin again. He doesn't tell her to give an offering for her healing or sprinkle holy water on her. He loves her unconditionally and shows her a new image of spiritual freedom that eventually brings healing to her heart, leading to a new identity. Jesus expresses the presence of God through relationship! Again, He demonstrates—no more veil. The woman said to Him:

> *"Our fathers worshiped on this mountain, and you Jews say that in Jerusalem is the place where one ought to worship." Jesus said to her, "Woman, believe Me, the hour is coming when you will neither on this mountain, nor in Jerusalem, worship the Father. You worship what you do not know; we know what we worship, for salvation is of the Jews. But the hour is coming, and now is, when the **true worshipers will worship the Father in spirit and truth; for the Father is seeking such to worship Him.** God is Spirit, and those who worship Him must worship in spirit and truth." The woman said to Him, "I know that Messiah is coming" (who is called Christ). "When He comes, He will tell us all things." Jesus said to her, "I who speak to you am He"* (John 4:20-26).

I am amazed by the love of God in action! The woman asked where the correct place was to go to worship, and Jesus settled it once and for all by telling her worship was no longer a place she would have to go to but that the place had come to her! Worship would no longer be about the temple in Jerusalem or the temple on Mount Gerizim, because the time was coming when she would be the temple.

No more worship from a distance—no more veil. Jesus told her the hour was coming when she would be able to have a personal Spirit-to-spirit relationship with the God of the universe whom Jesus introduced her to as "Father"! What? Wait a minute! She knew all kinds of names for God, but she had never ever heard God called Father; neither had anyone else before Jesus. In John 14:9, Jesus says, *"He who has seen Me has seen the Father."*

When Jesus told the woman that she didn't know the God of her worship, He made a profound statement, because not knowing who you worship always results in false worship and ignorant worship. We see it in the book of Acts:

> *Then Paul stood in the midst of the Areopagus and said, "Men of Athens, I perceive that in all things you are very religious; for as I was passing through and considering the objects of your worship, I even found an altar with this inscription: TO THE UNKNOWN GOD. Therefore, the One whom you worship without knowing, Him I proclaim to you: God, who made the world and everything in it, since He is Lord of heaven and earth,* ***does not dwell in temples made with hands. Nor is He worshiped with men's hands, as though He needed anything,*** *since He gives to all life, breath, and all things. And*

He has made from one blood every nation of men to dwell on all the face of the earth, and has determined their preappointed times and the boundaries of their dwellings (Acts 17:22-26).

When Jesus said to the woman that salvation was of the Jews in John 4:22, He was simply speaking of Himself as a Jewish man and her salvation; as a result, she would now be able to have a living relationship with a living God—the God she would know, but more importantly the God who would know her by name!

Jesus went on to tell the woman that the only way to have a relationship with God is in spirit and truth. Notice Jesus says true worshipers worship the Father in spirit and truth, or worship according to the Word of God as John 17:17 so clearly declares: *"Your Word is truth."* We have to worship according to the Word of God, not public opinion. Jesus didn't give us another way to worship or another helpful option or suggestion to have a relationship with God. *Jesus is the only way to the Father!* (See John 14:6.)

"You must worship in spirit and truth" is pretty clear, don't you think? He wants you! He wants to have a living relationship with you! *"For the eyes of the Lord run to and fro throughout the whole earth, to show Himself strong on behalf of those whose heart is loyal to Him"* (2 Chronicles 16:9). He is looking for you!

I have been involved in many worship conferences and seminars in my lifetime, and I remember years ago when people thought that true worshipers were the really expressive ones, the ones who moved their hands in the air in special circular motions and just seemed to be way more creative in worship than everyone else, or the people who were very outgoing and animated! They were the *true worshipers!*

Many people don't realize that everybody worships! Unbelievers worship, even though they don't worship the Father. Humans were designed to worship! To worship the Father, you have to have a spirit relationship with God, and the only way to do that is through Jesus. This is a *true worshiper!*

> *Jesus said to him, "I am the way, the truth, and the life. No one comes to the Father except through Me"* (John 14:6).
>
> *For through Him we both* [Jews and Gentiles] *have access by one Spirit to the Father* (Ephesians 2:18).
>
> *It is the Spirit who gives life; the flesh profits nothing. The words that I speak to you are spirit, and they are life* (John 6:63).

One of the acceptable tag lines when it comes to God is to be "a person of faith," which can literally mean anything in today's culture. You can be a person of faith and be any religion in the world and worship whoever or whatever you want and call it faith. Sadly, even unbelievers will call themselves Christians because they were born in America or because they are born into a religious family in any country. Some people worship money or their lifestyle status; some worship being worshiped; some worship sex, entertainment, or a job; and many bow their lives to any other image except the person of Christ.

All religions do *not* lead to God, and there are *not* multiple ways to have a relationship with God or to worship God. Jesus said that God is a Spirit and those who worship Him *must worship* in spirit and truth. Notice the Father is not seeking your worship; He is seeking you—those who will worship Him.

He is looking for you, and it doesn't matter how messed up your life is; He still wants you and sees your value even if you don't. Your future is not defined by your past. Your past is past! God's grace always erases it when you repent. God is just waiting for you to receive His grace for yourself. God is waiting.

When Jesus is speaking of worship to this woman at the well, the word He used for worship tells us so much about God's heart for us. It is a compound word, *pros-kuneo,* which means "toward" and to "kiss." The word picture is a face-to-face relationship. This was always what God wanted, but He could never have that desire fulfilled until Jesus came to earth to make it happen. Jesus came to reveal the Father and said we would worship the Father in spirit and truth.

Jesus is how we can worship face to face rather than through a representative or a veil of some kind. Nothing can separate us from the presence of God anymore! We can worship God the Father. The word Jesus used here for Father is the Greek word *pater,* or *ab* in Hebrew. The Aramaic word for Father is *abba,* and modern Hebrew today uses Abba or Papa, showing us an intimate, personal image of a loving Father.

For as many as are led by the Spirit of God, these are sons of God. For you did not receive the spirit of bondage again to fear, but you received the Spirit of adoption by whom we cry out, "Abba, Father" (Romans 8:14-15).

In the early 1990s, I had the opportunity to be part of the Integrity Music recording called "Shalom Jerusalem" in Israel with my friend Paul Wilbur. Another friend, Don Moen, and Pastor Jack and Anna Hayford were all on the tour as well. It was very special for me because Jack Hayford was my pastor while I lived in California from 1973–75, and Don Moen was in our worship orchestra, playing violin in the early '80s in Tulsa at a church then called Grace Fellowship, where I was the worship leader. Each of these people had a special place in my heart. I knew it was a moment in time that I would never forget.

As I went into the ancient city of Jerusalem one day near the Western Wall, I heard young children in the streets calling out to their dads, saying, "Abba, abba!" which translates, "Papa, papa!" I thought immediately of this passage and I wondered if my heart would burst with love. What kind of God would want us to call Him "Papa"? That name is so personal and is what Jesus came to show us. He wants us to have an intimate relationship with Him that will transform the way we live.

God doesn't love you back; He loved you first!

God wants us to know how loved we are, and we often mistakenly think that doing something spiritual will impress God into loving us in return. Ignorantly, somehow we think we can do something greater than Jesus laying down His life.

Really? I don't think so! What could be greater? Greater love has no one than to lay down his life for his friends.

> *But when the fullness of the time had come, God sent forth His Son, born of a woman, born under the law, to redeem those who were under the law, that we might receive the adoption as sons. And because you are sons, God has sent forth the Spirit of His Son **into your hearts,** crying out, "Abba, Father!" Therefore you are no longer a slave but a son, and if a son, then an heir of God through Christ* (Galatians 4:4-7).

My dad moved to heaven a couple of years ago as of this writing, at just a few months shy of being 97 years old. I saw him often because he was in a care facility in our city of Colorado Springs. The last time I saw him alert is a memory I will always cherish. He was sitting up in a wheelchair in the dining area, and as soon as he saw me he looked up and smiled real big. As I was approaching him, he threw open his arms to embrace me. When we embraced, he kissed me on my cheek and hugged me tight and told me how much he loved me and always would.

That is face to face, and that is our heavenly Father's desire for me and for you. Even if your earthly father has never or will never give you that moment on earth, your Abba Father is waiting for you with open arms, ready to welcome you into His family. I will be so glad to see my dad again someday. Until then, I worship God in spirit and in truth. The gift of perspective keeps on giving. It affects everything—not only how you see God but how you see life. When we worship from the outside in, we will always see through limitation!

Jesus said to the woman at the well:

> *"God is Spirit, and those who worship Him must worship in spirit and truth." The woman said to Him, "I know that Messiah is coming" (who is called Christ). "When He comes, He will tell us all things." Jesus said to her, "I who speak to you am He"* (John 4:24-26).

Always remember, divine appointments defy social barriers. Be prepared to welcome Jesus into your life right where you are. The woman's life perspective was changed for the better, for eternity.

4

PERSPECTIVE CHANGES EVERYTHING

I'm sure you have been in conversations when you have said, "Oh, I see." Saying that, we are essentially indicating that we understand what the other person said; we see the person's perspective about a situation. A person's perspective determines how someone acts, reacts, and responds to every situation. Their perspective is an accumulation of years of previous experiences.

Let's look at the story of Jesus at the well from the perspective of Jesus' disciples:

> *And at this point His disciples came, and they marveled that He talked with a woman; yet no one said,* "What do You seek?" *or,* "Why are You talking with her?" *The woman then left her waterpot, went her way into the city, and said to the men,* "Come, see a Man who told me all things that I ever did. Could*

*this be the Christ?" Then they went out of the city and came to Him. In the meantime His disciples urged Him, saying, "Rabbi, eat." But He said to them, "**I have food to eat of which you do not know.**" Therefore the disciples said to one another, "Has anyone brought Him anything to eat?" Jesus said to them, "**My food is to do the will of Him who sent Me, and to finish His work.** Do you not say, 'There are still four months and then comes the harvest'? Behold, I say to you, **lift up your eyes and look** at the fields, for they are already white for harvest! And he who reaps receives wages, and gathers fruit for eternal life, **that both he who sows and he who reaps may rejoice together.** For in this the saying is true: 'One sows and another reaps.' I sent you to reap that for which you have not labored; others have labored, and you have entered into their labors"* (John 4:27-38).

The disciples are returning from getting food when they see Jesus talking with the woman at the well. Like us so many times, they are not plugged into or connecting with what Jesus is doing. They are more concerned with public image and being politically correct than why He is talking to her. The disciples, daily followers of Jesus, haven't yet picked up on His leadership or compassion. They are more focused on the moment rather than the eternal perspective of what is happening. Much like us many times, instead of being disciples, they are being more like the duh-sciples! They see with natural eyes and ears, so their perspective is limited, and they limit God during this divine appointment by not opening their spiritual eyes and ears.

We need to "lift our eyes" or, in other words, we need to change our perspective so we can see what God sees. We often look at the unbeliever from a physical perspective and come up with an outcome that declares, "There are still four more months until they're ready." But in essence, Jesus is saying to the disciples, "No, *you're* not ready! You're more concerned with PR and food than you are with Kingdom culture, the image of God, and your identity as a disciple."

He is saying to them and us, "You need to get ready for the harvest by changing your perspective. Once you see it, you can be it. When you lift your eyes, give yourself permission to really look and see what is God seeing and doing and saying. Once you see with God's vision, you will have His perspective. God knows the harvest is ready; the harvest has been ready!"

Look at this demonstration of the love of God in Christ in Matthew 9:

> *Then Jesus went about all the cities and villages, teaching in their synagogues, preaching the gospel of the kingdom, and healing every sickness and every disease among the people. But when He saw the multitudes,* ***He was moved with compassion for them,*** *because they were weary and scattered, like sheep having no shepherd. Then He said to His disciples,* ***"The harvest truly is plentiful,*** *but the laborers are few. Therefore* ***pray the Lord of the harvest to send out laborers into His harvest"*** *(Matthew 9:35-38).*

It's easy to see the flaws and the limitations in the lives of the disciples, isn't it? I mean if this was your potential leadership team, what would you have seen? Would you have considered them qualified for ministry? When you look at the people around you even now, what do you see? Do you see problems or potential? What determines capacity? Do your current patterns determine your capacity, or is it more about getting God's perspective and discovering your true identity?

In the Gospels, Peter stepped out of the boat and began to sink in the sea, but at least he stepped out, right? As disciples, if we were ever arrested for being a follower of Jesus, would there be enough evidence to convict us? From the root comes the fruit, and the proof is the fruit. We don't have to strive to achieve what we're supposed to receive with thankfulness. In Christ, faith receives what grace has given.

REJOICING TOGETHER

In the middle of the conversation with the disciples after the woman at the well left and they returned from getting food, why did Jesus speak about the fields being ready for harvest, saying, *"that both he who sows and he who reaps may rejoice together"* (John 4:36)? That's kind of weird, isn't it? What does rejoicing together have to do with anything? This word for "rejoice" in the Greek means "to be cheerful," calmly happy, or to be glad, and literally to be able to say, "it is well with my soul."

In other words, God is saying during this amazing time of harvest—this time of the New Covenant, the church age, when our attitude, our soul, is filled with His perspective—no matter what is going on and whatever we are doing, whether it is planting or harvesting, we can have a calm assurance in our hearts that what we are doing matters. We, all together as planters and harvesters, should be exceedingly glad about what God is doing. Our lives as worshipers should reflect a cheerfulness that is communicated through how we live from the inside out. Rejoicing should be our normal lifestyle!

Colossians 3:17 says, *"And whatever you do in word or deed, do all in the name of the Lord Jesus, giving thanks to God the Father through Him."*

I don't know if you have ever planted a big garden, but I grew up with parents who loved to garden, and I'm married to a wonderful woman who also loves to garden. I can tell you planting is a lot of work, especially as you get the soil ready and prepared to receive the seed. But when that produce starts coming in, harvesting that fresh food is really fun, even though it's also a lot of work!

Your harvest will always be greater than your planted seed.

The time of harvest seems way more fun than the time of planting, but God says this time of grace that He has called us into is not like that; although one sows and another reaps, God is the One who gives the increase. Through grace we change our perspective. We partner with the God of the impossible, and God gives the increase! Is it possible that we are not thinking big enough? How much increase will God give?

*So then neither he who plants is anything, nor he who waters, **but God who gives the increase** (1 Corinthians 3:7).*

Don't worship the planter, the one who waters, or the harvester—instead, worship God.

THE HARVEST OF GRACE IS A TIME TO REJOICE TOGETHER

Amos, an Old Covenant prophet, prophesied about a harvest time yet to come that would find its fulfillment in the New Covenant, through you and me as the place of His grace.

> *"On that day I will raise up the tabernacle of David, which has fallen down, and repair its damages; I will raise up its ruins, and rebuild it as in the days of old; that they may possess the remnant of Edom, and all the Gentiles who are called by My name," says the Lord who does this thing. **"Behold, the days are coming," says the Lord, "when the plowman shall overtake the reaper, and the treader of grapes him who sows seed;** the mountains shall drip with sweet wine, and all the hills shall flow with it. I will bring back the captives of My people Israel; they shall build the waste cities and inhabit them; they shall plant vineyards and drink wine from them; they shall also make gardens and eat fruit from them. I will plant them in their land, and no longer shall they be pulled up from the land I have given them," says the Lord your God (Amos 9:11-15).*

Almost all prophecy has layers of application—both immediately for the people it was being spoken over historically, and spiritually it usually has a broader application. This passage from Amos is no exception. There are many other examples of this in Scripture, such as the prophecy of Joel in chapter 2 when Joel is speaking over Israel. However, in Acts 2 during the church age, when Peter is preaching using this passage in Joel 2:28-32, he applies it "spiritually" to what was taking place in that moment as the church was being birthed forth in power! I love how the Holy Spirit prophetically communicated that through him.

In this Amos passage, we see a very similar process. Amos was prophesying over the nation of Israel, historically speaking. However, look at the spiritual application here in this next passage:

> *And after they had become silent, James answered, saying, "Men and brethren, listen to me: Simon has declared how God at the first visited the Gentiles to take out of them a people for His name. And with this the words of the prophets agree, just as it is written: 'After this I will return and will rebuild the tabernacle of David, which has fallen down; I will rebuild its ruins, and I will set it up; so that the rest of mankind may seek the Lord, even all the Gentiles who are called by My name, says the Lord who does all these things'"* (Acts 15:13-17).

The apostle James, being led by the Spirit of God, confirms what they've been talking about in this whole Acts 15 passage by quoting the Amos 9:11-12 passage. Don't miss this—this is huge!

This is more significant than we can imagine, because it is all about the difference between the Old Covenant and New Covenant and how it impacts worship in our generation today! The Holy Spirit in the Acts 15 passage shows the contrast between the harvest that the law produces and the harvest that grace produces.

God always wanted a people He could meet with face to face and share His heart; however, Israel was afraid of God's presence, which isn't all that different for many people today, even Christians. For example, we often want someone we consider "more qualified" to tell us what God is saying instead of going to God directly.

> *Now all the people witnessed the thunderings, the lightning flashes, the sound of the trumpet, and the mountain smoking; and when the people saw it, they trembled and stood afar off. Then they said to Moses,* **"You speak with us, and we will hear; but let not God speak with us, lest we die."** *And Moses said to the people, "Do not fear; for God has come to test you, and that His fear may be before you, so that you may not sin."* **So the people stood afar off, but Moses drew near** *the thick darkness where God was* (Exodus 20:18-21).

God had given His Word on Mount Sinai in the form of the Ten Commandments to Israel through Moses. Eventually over time, there were 613 laws that had to be followed that would teach them right from wrong, how to obey, and even how to worship.

During this time period in history, God instituted a plan where a physical dwelling place called a tabernacle would show them *an image* on a daily basis. It was a graphic visual so they would eventually acknowledge that they could not fulfill the law perfectly and confess their need for a Savior.

Under this covenant they would be required to bring animal sacrifices for their sins. These animals would have to be slain, shedding blood. Priests would represent them before God, and a high priest would make atonement for their sins once a year. All of this was intentional to help them gain perspective, so the people could see what was required to be in relationship with God. God communicated an image that would especially show them their need for a Lamb of God, a Savior, a Messiah.

So what is a "tabernacle" exactly? A tabernacle is a dwelling place or just simply a tent. When Israel was a nomadic people, God had them set up a huge "tent of meeting," especially in their early years as a nation, called the tabernacle of Moses, where He could meet with Moses. God gave specific instructions and meticulous requirements and was very expressive and artistic in the details of this tabernacle. This was so they would begin to see that they could never be good enough or holy enough to earn their way to right standing with God. As they went from place to place in the desert, through the animal sacrifice and being obedient to the law in order to experience blessing instead of cursing, even the most righteous among them would discover they could not be good enough. God wanted them to know that He was the only One who was perfect and always good!

God wanted them to discover that there was no way they could do the law perfectly! They could never be justified by their works, which was the whole purpose of the law. As Galatians clearly points out, the law was a schoolmaster to bring them to Christ—to bring them into the grace of God. God had something so much better in mind, but it was yet for an appointed time.

Moses' tabernacle was set up by God. In Israel's history, shortly after crossing the Red Sea, even though it took time, God used their journey to eventually bring them into another tabernacle—the tabernacle of David.

David built houses for himself in the City of David; and he prepared a place for the ark of God, and pitched a tent for it (1 Chronicles 15:1).

In this Old Covenant time frame, they had to go to God, but in the New Covenant God came to us! An entirely different perspective of His presence.

The tabernacle of David was a foreshadowing of an amazing picture of God's grace because there was no outer court and no inner court, only the Ark of the Covenant that was in plain sight for all to see so they could worship 24/7 in front of the presence of God. During this time of the tabernacle of David, Jews and Gentiles from conquered nations came together. The young, old, male, and female came together to worship in celebration of the Lord of the harvest with great rejoicing. This was where David danced before the Lord with all his might!

The tabernacle of David was a sign or a prophetic picture of the harvest of grace that was going to come, confirmed in Acts 15. The church is the expression of God's presence today just like David's tabernacle was back in the time of David, with one major difference: the presence was upon them, in their midst, and for us today the presence is within us and flows out of us in living water! We are the place of His dwelling! We are the body of Christ!

> *And with this the words of the prophets agree, just as it is written: "After this I will return and will rebuild the tabernacle of David, which has fallen down; I will rebuild its ruins, and I will set it up; so that the rest of mankind may seek the Lord, even all the Gentiles who are called by My name, says the Lord who does all these things"* (Acts 15:15-17).
>
> *For we are the circumcision, who worship God in the Spirit, rejoice in Christ Jesus, and have no confidence in the flesh* (Philippians 3:3).

THIS IS OUR TIME

The church on earth is the place of God's presence. We are the temple, we are the dwelling, we are the body of Christ. We are the tabernacle of David rebuilt and restored through Christ, King David's Greater Son! In the relationship of Christ and the church we see the expression of His presence on earth today. It is so important that we really get this, because we are literally the dwelling place of God on earth. We are the people of God, and because we are alive in the Spirit and we now have

His Word inside us, we are going into the harvest fields with the good news of the gospel. We are going to where the people are; we are going to where people live—we are not just expecting them to come to us. We are doing what Jesus did when He went to Samaria.

People worldwide are so ready to hear the good news of the gospel. John 4:35 says, *"Behold, I say to you, lift up your eyes and look at the fields, for they are already white for harvest!"* What the writer is saying here is that as you plant the seed of the gospel of grace into someone's heart, they are saying "yes" to this good news and taking it in. You will see the immediate harvest from your planted seed. This is the harvest of grace, not the harvest of legalism.

I believe God has called us as the church to be in perpetual harvest and perpetual planting, and one is overtaking the other to where the harvest will be so ready that we will not be able to contain it! The hills will drip with sweet wine—the blessing of the Lord will be upon the land that we enter. From God's perspective and according to John 4:36, wherever we go, blessing will follow. It is a great time of rejoicing!

Jesus made the bold statement that He would build His church and that the gates, the entrances, of hell would not prevail against His church. He is building His church through us, inside of people who believe. We are now literally manifesting God's abiding presence from the inside out.

Psalmist David says in Psalm 139:7-8, *"Where can I go from Your Spirit? Or where can I flee from Your presence? If I ascend into heaven, You are there; if I make my bed in hell* [in the underworld], *behold, You are there."*

But David did not have the presence of God living in him, nor did Isaiah or anyone from the Old Covenant. They had the Holy Spirit of God come on them, but they were not "born again" and they didn't have the Spirit of God living in them. The presence of God was finally able to be an abiding presence inside humanity only because of Christ, but that didn't happen and wasn't even possible until the death of Jesus and His glorious resurrection. Jesus became the fulfillment of the law so we could experience His grace and live in Him. He launched the New Covenant!

Jesus said, *"I will never leave you or forsake you"* (Hebrews 13:5).

Remember again what Jesus told the woman at the well about living water. He said that the living water would become in us a fountain of water springing up into everlasting life. He then confirmed it in John 7:38-39 when He made clear that *"out of the heart will flow rivers of living water.' But this He spoke concerning the Spirit, whom those believing in Him would receive; for the Holy Spirit was not yet given, because Jesus was not yet glorified."*

What started as revelation was replaced by imitation!

Now because of the Holy Spirit of God, this supernatural presence being in us, He is able to flow out of our spirit in rivers of living water. We can release God's presence or manifest it anytime, anywhere!

We are His dwelling place now! Since *"grace and truth came through Jesus Christ"* (John 1:17), we can partner with the Holy

Spirit, cooperate with Him as our Helper, and literally manifest the glory of God in our lifestyle and through our hearts on a daily basis.

Jesus wants us as His body, His church, His followers to be doing the same works He did, "His mighty works" which include signs and wonders and what the Bible refers to as the "greater works" He told us to do. Now these works are literally happening worldwide, not just through One Man, Jesus, fully man and fully God, being physically on the earth. Now, because of the work of God's grace, the body of Christ is all around the world! (See John 14:12.)

The grace of God through us has given new expression to the presence of God worldwide. His presence is flowing out of us, out of our hearts, out of our mouths, through our hands, and through our lives. Knowing how loved we are has produced compassion for people. Worshipers all around the world are learning how to give what was freely given to them, and together we are experiencing a great time of rejoicing. While the grace harvest is ready, many believers have not been ready. We need to respond and get ready and do what Jesus said to the fishermen who had been fishing all night.

> *Simon Peter said to them, "I am going fishing." They said to him, "We are going with you also." They went out and immediately got into the boat, and that night* **they caught nothing.** *But when the morning had now come, Jesus stood on the shore; yet the disciples did not know that it was Jesus.* **Then Jesus said to them,** *"Children, have you any food?" They answered*

*Him, "No." And He said to them, **"Cast the net on the right side of the boat, and you will find some." So they cast, and now they were not able to draw it in because of the multitude of fish*** (John 21:3-6).

Even the disciples as fishers of men had only seen limited success in their harvest. They had seen the Kingdom of God manifest, but they had placed limitations on God due to their unbelief—just like we have, many times! We have to start where we are instead of where we want to be. As you grab hold of this truth, it will change you and change your perspective. When God gives you a word, that is all you need to change everything. One word from God changes everything!

Jesus spoke His word to them to let down their nets on the other side. Don't ever go to the other side without a word from God. Just one word from God will change everything. Like Mary, the mother of Jesus, said at the wedding in Cana, *"Whatever He says to you, do it"* (John 2:5). (You thought Nike came up with that, didn't you?)

> **When they did what Jesus told them to do, everything changed!**

Maybe in your current storm, you're feeling like the disciples in the boat who thought they were going to get stuck in the middle of the storm and drown. Jesus said in Mark 4:35, *"On the same day, when evening had come, He said to them, 'Let us cross over to the other side.'"* Here is another example of a word from God mentioning the "other side." You are not going to fail; rather, you are going to the other side.

Even as the storm arose and the disciples all thought they were going to die, God knew otherwise. We go through storms in life and the enemy wants us to think that God somehow doesn't care. The disciples said, *"Teacher, do You not care?"* (Mark 4:38). And so have we! Instead of being fearful and entering into unbelief, remember what He says to you. When you have a word from God, it doesn't mean there won't be opposition or resistance, but when the storms come, and they will, remember you have a word—you are going to the other side! His Word will always trump your reality. He is greater!

When the disciples woke him up, Jesus spoke what He heard and what He believed, and the wind and sea obeyed Jesus! That's why He said to the storm, "Peace, be still!" Remember, Jesus only said what the Father told Him to say. Jesus tells us in Mark 11:23-24 that we as believers could also speak to mountains to be removed and cast into the sea! Storms and mountains have ears!

We are going to come up against situations where we need to know that we can impact the physical, the natural, from the authority given to us in Jesus' name. God loves it when we partner with the Holy Spirit and we speak His Word from a believing heart. If we want to partner with Him like this, we should not doubt in our heart, but rather believe that what we say will be done. When we say what He said from a believing heart, we will see obstacles removed and cast into the sea.

Even when you pray, Jesus said to believe that you receive whatever things you ask for and you will have them. Why would you pray otherwise? I'm asking for God's will to be done on earth as it is in heaven. I want to see the Kingdom invade every area of earth to the glory of God! What if right now, today, we saw the answer to that prayer? I really don't think we would be ready, do you?

We need to get ready, because right now our nets, our systems, would break if we had a huge harvest of grace. Ask the disciples! They couldn't pull in all their harvest that day because they were only using one net. When they called their partners to come help them, even then their nets began to break. Nets with holes don't work well! Likewise, our current systems, programs, our gatherings would not be able to handle the harvest because we haven't prepared our *hearts* for the grace harvest.

Isn't it interesting to see that the boundaries get closer as the time of the New Covenant approaches? Moses led to David who led to Jesus, who led to the Holy Spirit living in us.

Look what happened when the Holy Ghost manifested at the very beginning of the church age:

> *Then Peter said to them, "Repent, and let every one of you be baptized in the name of Jesus Christ for the remission of sins; and you shall receive the gift of the Holy Spirit. For the promise is **to you and to your children, and to all who are afar off, as many as the Lord our God will call.**" And with many other words he testified and exhorted them, saying, "Be saved from this perverse [crooked] generation." Then those who gladly received his word were baptized; and that day*

*about **three thousand souls** were added to them. And they continued steadfastly in the apostles' doctrine [teaching] and fellowship, in the breaking of bread, and in prayers. Then fear [awe] came upon every soul, and many wonders and signs were done through the apostles* (Acts 2:38-43).

Acts 2:47 ends with, *"And the Lord added to the church daily those who were being saved."*

Aren't you glad we don't have to wait for Him to show up? He's already here—in you and in me!

It's time, however, that we show up and then go out into the harvest fields. Go connect with people! The Bible never says God is looking for missionaries—He is looking for worshipers. If we have His heart, we will want to go into all the world!

We are entering a time of rejoicing, even in a culture filled with sin and adversity, when we will see the planter and the harvester rejoice together. Don't ever forget that where sin abounds, grace abounds much more! Great grace will cause great joy to flow throughout the land, and righteousness will exalt nation after nation as we go in the power of the Holy Spirit and in the love of God. I'm telling you, we are going to see huge numbers coming to Christ on a daily or perpetual basis—and it's going to cause great rejoicing! Prepare your heart and make room inside out now by worshiping in spirit and truth!

When you lift your eyes, you will see life with a new perspective. Let's return to our story about Jesus at the well in John 4 to see how this applies.

And many of the Samaritans of that city believed in Him because of the word of the woman who testified, "He told me all that I ever did" (John 4:39).

The love of God being demonstrated through the life of Jesus by loving them and speaking truth to them was so powerful that when the Samaritans had come to Him, they urged Him to stay with them. We must know the rhythms of grace so that we know when to move on or when it's time to stay a little longer.

*So when the Samaritans had come to Him, they urged Him to stay with them; and He stayed there two days. And many more believed because of **His own word**. Then they said to the woman, "Now we believe, not because of what you said, for we ourselves have heard Him and we know that this is indeed the Christ, the Savior of the world. Now **after the two days** He departed from there and went to Galilee* (John 4:40-43).

I find it very significant that Jesus the Christ, whose very name means "The Anointed One," was not afraid of being with these people or afraid of losing His anointing or being tainted by their humanity. The presence of God was being expressed through relationship one life at a time. Love never needs to fear sin! The love of God casts out all fear—even the fear believers often have of being around "sinners." Please be around sinners, showing them God's love through you. There is no fear in love. (See 1 John 4:18.) Change your perspective and you can change people lives for Christ.

The phrase "He stayed there two days" should minister such a headline to us as believers, as followers of Jesus, as disciples today. Even though the Samaritans were considered by the Jews to be enemies, or "problem people" at the very least and an untouchable people by most, Jesus not only was led there in a divine appointment that defied social barriers, but because He ministered the love of God to them first, and then spoke truth to them second, they believed Him.

Then their perspective changed and they asked Jesus to stay with them, and He did for two more days. When Jesus stayed, I've always wondered what the disciples did for those two days. Did they leave? Where did they go? And what did Jesus do and say during those two days?

It is so important for us to discern the seasons and what God is saying, because in the beginning of Jesus' ministry, Jesus told the disciples not to go into Samaria!

> *These twelve Jesus sent out and commanded them, saying: "Do not go into the way of the Gentiles, and do not enter a city of the Samaritans. But go rather to the lost sheep of the house of Israel"* (Matthew 10:5-6).

Why did Jesus tell them that at the beginning of their new assignment to follow Him but not to go to the Gentiles and specifically not to go to Samaria? They weren't ready! They hadn't had time to prepare their hearts yet. Jesus was showing them that timing is everything, thus revealing to us that preparation is a key to manifestation.

When Jesus was first talking to the woman at the well, the disciples eventually returned from going to get some food for everyone. However, we don't really know what happened to them after they brought Jesus the food, because we don't hear anything about them until the topic of food is brought up again in John 6 when they were feeding the five thousand people gathered to hear Jesus teach. We don't really know where the disciples eventually slipped off to, but what we do know for sure is that Jesus stayed—for two more days.

We're going to see from the Word that the Jews falsely accused Jesus of being a Samaritan, perhaps because He was from Nazareth, a city just north of Mount Gerizim. Perhaps there was something else also, like guilt by association, because in just a couple of chapters from this time in the John 4 passage we discover something very interesting about the religious reaction to His time in Samaria.

I believe because Jesus, being led by the Holy Spirit, dared to defy the Samaritan social barrier through a divine appointment, the religious Jews accused Him of being one of the Samaritans; they couldn't think of anything worse to say to Jesus because they hated the Samaritans.

John 8:48 says, *"Then the Jews answered and said to Him, 'Do we not say rightly that You are a Samaritan and have a demon?'"* Oh wow, this is just like the enemy!

When you are a worshiper, you will be called into many divine appointments that defy social barriers, and many times even the religious people of our day will accuse you of giving a license to sin or that you are somehow approving of their sin by ministering to them. Don't worry about it; you are in good company—they said the same thing about Jesus! When you love people who are living in sin, you are not loving what they're doing or how they are living; you are loving the person. This is what God's love is all about!

Sadly, the religious legalists often think that loving someone is approving their behavior. Love is not saying I approve of everything you do, but I do love you in spite of what you do. God did it first!

Romans 5:8 makes it clear that God loved us while we were still sinners, and Christ died for us while we were still sinners—so why wouldn't we love the harvest that God loves? Jesus demonstrated God's love to the Samaritan people, and even though the Jews had no dealings with them, Jesus, the Son of God, did! Jesus Himself, under divine direction, sowed into the people of Samaria, and later that sown seed was harvested with God giving the increase. Look at this:

> *Therefore those who were scattered went everywhere preaching the word. Then Philip went down to the city of Samaria and preached Christ to them. And the multitudes with one accord heeded the things spoken by Philip, hearing and seeing the miracles which he did. For unclean spirits, crying with a loud voice, came out of many who were possessed; and many who were paralyzed and lame were healed. And there was great joy in that city* (Acts 8:4-8).

This divine encounter was so important to the heart of God that the people of Samaria are now included in the Great Commission! (See Acts 1:8.)

God sees value in all people and cares to send His very best! Jesus, the Word made flesh, the One who was and is even before time existed, now submits to the Samaritans' repeated requests for more time with them. By saying yes, Jesus revealed this divine appointment defying social barriers—which changed their perspective of Him and Jews. This is what the love of God does! Jesus shows us what the culture of grace looks like—and what amazing grace it is!

What happened during those two more days? Jesus revealed His heavenly Father's love to the Samaritans and invited them into the Kingdom of God. Their perspective was changed—for eternity.

5

THERE'S SOMETHING ABOUT DAILY LIFE

See then that you walk circumspectly [carefully], *not as fools but as wise, redeeming the time, because the days are evil* (Ephesians 5:15-16).

This is the day that the Lord has made; we will rejoice and be glad in it (Psalm 118:24).

Then He came to the disciples and found them sleeping, and said to Peter, "What! Could you not watch with Me one hour? Watch and pray, lest you enter into temptation. The spirit indeed is willing, but the flesh is weak" (Matthew 26:40-41).

Even though it was the mid-1980s, I remember as if it were yesterday. A well-known minister named Larry Lea released a teaching titled "Could You Not Tarry One Hour?" that became very popular. It was a great teaching and his intent was to help people come into a more meaningful prayer life by spending the first hour of each day in a systematic prayer routine. This was primarily done by going through the Lord's Prayer in segments with lots of Scripture to pray out loud. Out of twenty-four hours in a day, from this Scripture in Matthew, the idea was for believers to commit to one hour with God in prayer.

I know many people were helped tremendously in their prayer life, but for some, including me, systematic turned into routine. The system was great, but as you will see something "not so great" was happening in my heart.

> *Now in the morning, having risen a long while before daylight, He [Jesus] went out and departed to a solitary place; and there He prayed. And Simon and those who were with Him searched for Him. When they found Him, they said to Him, "Everyone is looking for You" (Mark 1:35-37).*

Everyone was looking for me, too, but not for the same reasons! I was already a person of prayer, and in those early years I had studied prayer under Dick Eastman and several other teachers. So when this teaching came out, I was determined to give God my first hour of each day, come hell or high water! I remember how hard it was to wake up that early and start praying and make sense of what I was saying at first. I really did want to spend time with Jesus, I loved Him with my whole heart, and I was trying to tell Him that.

However, it wasn't even ten minutes into my early morning hour when I started repeating random sentences or pieces of sentences that really didn't make any sense. Then I didn't even realize that I had fallen asleep—several times I woke up drooling. It was not pretty, but neither was my bed head that early in the morning.

Here I was calling Jesus my best Friend and thanking Him for His love for me during my prayer, and the next minute I was asleep—not too different from the disciples, right? Then, one time, I thought I was really making progress because just like Jesus, everyone was looking for me—but not because I was praying, but because I was sleeping. I felt like a failure! I was trying so hard to love Jesus. I didn't really know yet that I still needed to experience how much He loved me. I was trying so hard to *do* for Him that I was failing at *being with* Him. I had put myself under the law again!

I started to value more what I was trying so hard to do, rather than what Jesus had already done!

I got so frustrated with my prayer life that I halfheartedly tried to make a deal with Jesus by telling Him that we could both save ourselves a bunch of time, as I basically said the same thing every day. I told Him it would be a lot more effective if I just recorded my hour of prayer on a cassette tape (it was the mid-80s) and just play that cassette every morning. It was a pretty stupid idea, and I knew better than to try to make my relationship with Jesus some kind of "let's make a deal, Jesus," but I'm pretty sure I made Him laugh!

At least now I knew how the disciples must have felt when Jesus asked why they couldn't stay awake and pray for an hour.

What was I going to do about a whole day if I couldn't even do an hour? I felt like such a pitiful Christian. I mean, who can't pray for a least an hour early in the morning!?

My spiritual time management was flawed. I was telling a close friend about my frustration, and he said, "I know what you mean; this dying thing is killing me!" We both laughed until we were crying! What really will kill you, however, is when you've made your life about living *for* God instead of living *in* Him. When the focus is on you, and you're still trying to die all the time, what you're not doing gets watered down with religion and law. Instead of doing because of how loved you are by God and that faith works by love, you *do* to prove you have faith! Somehow my redeemed spirit knew, even if my mind didn't get it yet, that life is about living, not dying! I started to understand that my spirit was being renewed day to day!

> *For it is all for your sake, so that as grace extends to more and more people it may increase thanksgiving, to the glory of God. So we do not lose heart. Though our outer self is wasting away, our inner self is being* **renewed day by day** (2 Corinthians 4:15-16 ESV).

I heard someone say recently that what you do every day matters more than what you do once in a while! I really like that, and the Word of God confirms that idea by saying we need to be renewed inwardly day by day—not Sunday to Sunday or conference to conference. Isn't it amazing how day by day adds up to year by year? If you don't like the life you're living and want different results, you can't keep doing the same things every day in the same ways. You must renew, change, and transform.

Every long-term goal begins with small daily habits that have a way of adding up. Don't wait to start until you have it all figured out or you'll never start. You can't expect to arrive if you never begin. What if you really believed in your heart that you needed to be renewed day by day? How would life change for you? Andrew Wommack says, "You may not have arrived, but thank God you've left!"

I believe the Holy Spirit will help us learn to seize the day and live each day to the fullest and for His glory! When Jesus called us to be in a face-to-face relationship as true worshipers who worship Him in spirit and truth, Jesus said true worshipers *must* worship this way, but how do we do this day by day? Most people think that worship is something done once a week in a church building, instead of realizing they are the building and God has called them into something that happens day by day!

THE SOUND OF HEAVEN

Another memory of the early '80s is a cassette tape on which someone had somehow captured the "sound of heaven" on a recording. If I remember correctly, it was supposed to have been recorded during a meeting where angels were singing and the people could hear them. I was excited to hear it, because I was in a meeting personally when we actually did hear what seemed like the sound of angels singing with us—it was incredible, anointed, and powerful! The person who gave me the cassette was so excited for me to hear it.

The synthesizer was then a new electronic musical instrument that had various new sounds never heard before. We were just starting to find new expressions for the synthesizer as an instrument of worship in the church. Some of the more popular early usages included sounds that were of string sections, and what we would describe as angels' voices or heavenly sounds. When I played the cassette, it sounded exactly like some of those new sound selections on the synthesizer. It was nice, and it was new, but it didn't sound heavenly like they had described.

The longer I listened the more depressed I felt! I wondered, *What if this really is the sound of heaven? What if this is what it's really going to be like when I get there?* I could barely stand a few minutes of this boring "Ah" sound, let alone for eternity. I wasn't sure I wanted to go to heaven anymore if this was the sound of heaven!

Just before I was about to jump off the cliff, I felt the Lord tell me to wake up and read Revelation 5. He said, "I told you what heaven sounds like!"

I said out loud, "You did?"

The Spirit of God said to me, "I told you the sound of heaven is the sound of redeemed earth!"

> And **they sang a new song, saying**: "You are worthy to take the scroll, and to open its seals; for You were slain, and have redeemed us to God by Your blood out of every tribe and tongue and people and nation, and have made us kings and priests to our God; and we shall reign on the earth."

*Then I looked, and I heard the voice of many angels around the throne, the living creatures, and the elders; and the number of them was ten thousand times ten thousand, and thousands of thousands, **saying** with a loud voice: "**Worthy is the Lamb who was slain to receive power and riches and wisdom, and strength and honor and glory and blessing!**"*

*And every creature which is in heaven and on the earth and under the earth and such as are in the sea, and all that are in them, I heard **saying**: "**Blessing and honor and glory and power be to Him who sits on the throne, and to the Lamb, forever and ever!**" Then the four living creatures said, "Amen!" And the twenty-four elders fell down and worshiped Him who lives forever and ever* (Revelation 5:9-14).

Look at what the Spirit of God wrote for us about how more than 100 million angels and every creature in heaven and on earth and even in the sea worship using words—they were "saying," not just emitting the sound of a high pitched "Ah."

I was so encouraged! I knew heaven was going to be amazing in ways beyond what I could even imagine, including the worship. I also knew that Jesus had taught the disciples to pray for the will of God to be done on earth as it is in heaven. Could we actually be experiencing the will of God on earth in our lifetime even as the will of God is being done in heaven? Could we actually experience worship on earth as it is in heaven—now in our everyday lives?

Luke 11:2-3 says, *"So He said to them, 'When you pray, say: Our Father in heaven, hallowed be Your name; Your kingdom come. Your will be done on earth as it is in heaven. Give us this day* [or day by day] *our daily bread.'"* I told you there's something about life that is so daily!

What if what we do every day really does matter and living this life in Christ in "our lifetime of time" happens day by day? What if we are missing something really big by living from convention to convention, from seminar to seminar, from event to event instead of from day to day?

Do you feel like you just don't have enough hours in the day? I have felt that way many times. "If I just had more time," we often say or hear said. Obviously, time management is an important topic and there are many things we can do to have a more productive day, but did you know the major limitation is how we think about our time? If you have a positive attitude toward time, instead of contributing to the negative cycle of "not enough" and the lie of "lack," you will find time as a friend instead of an enemy. Instead of trying to do everything quickly, what if we just did what we did well. If we make time our friend, we could say more often, "It is well with my soul." Tick tock, tick tock. Sunrise, sunset.

Jesus brings value to every day, and the Word of God teaches us that there is a better covenant today with better promises, so there must be a better way to live and to worship. We get to live life in Him from day to day!

LIVING IN HIM

God, the Creator of the universe, sent His beloved Son to be born as a tiny baby, all in the fullness of time. Infinite became finite. Eternal became flesh. Deity became human. It was all for us!

If we live in the Spirit, let us also walk in the Spirit (Galatians 5:25).

Nicodemus said to Him, "How can a man be born when he is old? Can he enter a second time into his mother's womb and be born?" Jesus answered, "Most assuredly, I say to you, unless one is born of water and the Spirit, he cannot enter the kingdom of God. That which is born of the flesh is flesh, and that which is born of the Spirit is spirit. Do not marvel that I said to you, 'You must be born again'" (John 3:4-7).

Now when He was asked by the Pharisees when the kingdom of God would come, He answered them and said, "The kingdom of God does not come with observation; nor will they say, 'See here!' or 'See there!' For indeed, the kingdom of God is within you" (Luke 17:20-21).

*Which none of the rulers of this age knew; for had they known, they would not have crucified the Lord of glory. But as it is written: "**Eye has not seen, nor ear heard, nor have entered into the heart of man the things which God has prepared for those who love Him.**" But God has revealed them to us through His*

Spirit. For the Spirit searches all things, yes, the deep things of God (1 Corinthians 2:8-10).

Listen—if you are born again, your human spirit inside you is what was born again. Your human spirit is what makes you human; it is what makes you a created being. Being born again by the Spirit of God is what makes you a brand-new creation.

God has made the Kingdom of God available to you and placed it within you. Because you are now living in the Spirit, by the Spirit you really can do life in the Spirit. Your whole life can be lived to the glory of God, even in common every-day things—especially in common everyday things!

Therefore, whether you eat or drink, or whatever you do, do all to the glory of God (1 Corinthians 10:31).

Living life in Christ is not just giving Him first place but letting Him be the center of our entire life. I finally began to discover why it had been so hard trying to live *for* Him; my own effort was exhausting. As I began learning how to live *in Him,* what seemed distant became present-tense and transformational.

For in Him we live and move and have our being (Acts 17:28).

*For **of Him and through Him and to Him are all things**, to whom be glory forever. Amen* (Romans 11:36).

I felt like God was letting me know there was a quality of life that He came to give believers now, while on earth! His presence is going to be amazing when we all get to heaven, no doubt, but the minute we are born again our eternity with Him has already begun. We don't need to wait to live a quality life in Christ until we get to heaven. Being in Christ *now* is what gives us quality of life, not stuff!

> *The thief does not come except to steal, and to kill, and to destroy. I have come that they may have life, and that they may have it more abundantly* (John 10:10). *For all the promises of God* **in Him** *are Yes, and in Him Amen, to the glory of God through us* (2 Corinthians 1:20).

In Christ, every promise is already a *yes*, and God has come to give us an amazing life *now* with heaven on earth, even in the midst of trouble and heartache. Jesus said to be of good cheer! Jesus conquered the enemy and then gave us His victory so that we could live life as more than conquerors (John 16:33).

> *Beware, brethren, lest there be in any of you an evil heart of unbelief in departing from the living God;* **but exhort** [encourage] **one another daily, while it is called "Today,"** *lest any of you be hardened through the deceitfulness of sin* (Hebrews 3:12-13).

How can we encourage each other day by day if we don't stay connected day by day? We have to come to a place where we see that *God's presence is always communicated through relationship.*

FACE TO FACE, DAY BY DAY

Jesus came to show us the Father, and God wants an intimate relationship with us to where we are living in a communion of a face-to-face relationship because of spirit and truth. God has never even thought about being distant and not present. We never need to feel like we are bothering Him because of all the people He has to deal with, as if you just have a few minutes to get your time in with Him. Jesus brought you into a face-to-face intimacy with God as your heavenly Father. There is no more distance; nothing will ever separate you from His love and presence.

I remember when I was a kid, I anticipated reading the "funny paper" as we called it—the cartoon page of the newspaper. I especially like the cartoon created by Bil Keane called *The Family Circus*. Not only did he address daily life scenarios we all experience, but he often celebrated them. I still enjoy his life work even today. Bil is now credited with a quote that I remember reading years ago and still love: "Yesterday is history, tomorrow a mystery, today is a gift, that's why it's called the present."

I love the idea of time being a gift! However, so many times I have been guilty of saying I don't have enough time! But the truth is, we have the same number of hours per day that everyone in history had. There are 24 hours in every day, and life happens a day at a time—*there's something about life that's so daily!*

It's not that people like Michelangelo, Leonardo da Vinci, or even Albert Einstein had more time than you and I do, but the time they spent had a huge impact on humanity for varied reasons, whether artistically, scientifically, or for whatever reason.

I remember in Tulsa when one of my fellow staff members at Grace Church said to me one day in a conversation, "There's something about life that's so daily." I thought it was funny at the time, and we both laughed together at the obvious truth, but I have grown to appreciate the true depth and value of that statement. I have owned it for so many years and I consider it mine now. It's something that I share often because of the power of the message.

Years later, when I was serving on a different church staff, my senior pastor would often say about something unpleasant or difficult, "In twenty-four hours it'll all be over." That would often help him get through a tough situation. The day he shared it with me, I was going through a challenging circumstance. He told me that difficult circumstances are like storms. Storms come and go, and the best part about storms is that they never last forever. I'm still thankful for that down-home advice today!

As a worshiper, I began to think about how important this concept of "the daily" really is, and when I saw it confirmed in the Word of God, I knew there was something more the Lord was showing me.

SMALL BEGINNINGS

My wife, Tracy, and I pioneered a church in the late 1990s. After a couple of years, there was one weekend when things had been particularly challenging, so we took a short retreat in the mountains at a huge retreat center. When we arrived, almost everyone who had been there for an event was in the process of leaving. We were the only ones at the center except for a couple of the on-site staff. It was great; the quiet was so refreshing and the alone time with each other was so needed.

We thought it would be fun to watch a video in the media room, so we put a movie in the VCR (remember those?) called *What About Bob?* It was a new movie at the time featuring Bill Murray, who played an obsessive-compulsive narcissistic patient of a self-involved psychiatrist named Dr. Leo Marvin, played by Richard Dreyfuss. Bill Murray, "Bob," lets Dr. Leo Marvin know right away, "I have problems!" Of course, the only help for him ever being normal is going to come from the brilliant mind of Dr. Leo Marvin. Among many situations that go badly, Dr. Marvin plans to brag about his new book called *Baby Steps* on a morning news show. It all goes very wrong!

This was one of the funniest movies we had ever seen and we laughed so hard we nearly hurt ourselves! A merry heart was the medicine that we needed to help us experience refreshment and rest from some of the craziness of ministry life and pastoring. It helped us put things back in perspective, and the time together alone became a fun memory that we will always treasure.

But there really was something powerful about the idea of "baby steps" that the movie presented—the idea of just starting where you are and taking the first step. Then take the next step, baby steps, and start moving forward one step at a time. Even though it was a movie, the idea stuck with us.

This idea of baby steps or, in other words, small steps in this journey we call life is really how it works, which is probably why the movie was so funny to us. There really is something about life that's so daily!

Great things come from small beginnings. Every great vision has a beginning. Lao-tzu, an ancient Chinese philosopher, is quoted as saying, "A journey of a thousand miles begins with a single step."

From small beginnings come great things! The Bible declares in Zechariah 4:10: *"For who has despised the day of small things?"*

And after all, no one thought anything good could come out of Nazareth: *"And Nathanael said to him, 'Can anything good come out of Nazareth?' Philip said to him, 'Come and see'"* (John 1:46).

Bethlehem had a similar reputation. How could Someone who changed history be born in Bethlehem and come from such a small beginning? God delights in bringing big things from small beginnings!

> *But you, Bethlehem Ephrathah, though* **you are little among the thousands** *of Judah, yet out of you shall come forth to Me the One to be Ruler in Israel, whose goings forth are from of old, from everlasting* (Micah 5:2).

God is timeless. He is not defined by time! He has always been and will always be. God is eternal from everlasting to everlasting. God created time for *our* benefit. There was no such thing as time before God created time, just like there was no such thing as light before God created light. The beginning was the beginning of matter, space, and time; but even before time, the great I AM, God Himself, was in eternity. He has always been! (See Genesis 1:1; Psalm 90:2.)

The Word stepped from eternity into time to bring us into eternity with Him. What amazing love! God has always existed in eternity and always will, but now because of the Word, Jesus, becoming flesh and living and dying for us, through His sacrifice He gave us the opportunity to become brand-new creations and live forever with Him! If we would just believe it and receive it. He stepped into time for us!

> *In the beginning was the Word, and the Word was with God, and the Word was God. He was in the beginning with God. All things were made through Him, and without Him nothing was made that was made* (John 1:1-3).

Our eternity spiritually in Christ has already begun if we are disciples, followers of Jesus. We're not human beings having a *spiritual* experience. We're spiritual beings having a *human* experience—and it happens day by day.

Unbelievers are people made in the image of God as well. If they do not receive what Jesus provides for them, deciding to go their own way instead of *the Way*, they will live forever, but separated from the love of God. They have rejected the only provision for their eternity with God.

> *That if you **confess** with your mouth the Lord Jesus and **believe** in your heart that God has raised Him from the dead, **you will be saved**. For with the heart one believes unto righteousness, and with the mouth confession is made unto salvation* (Romans 10:9-10). *Therefore, if anyone is in Christ, he is **a new creation**; old things have passed away; behold, all things have become new* (2 Corinthians 5:17).

He who believes in the Son has everlasting life; and he who does not believe the Son shall not see life, but the wrath of God abides on him (John 3:36).

And these [unbelievers] *will go away into everlasting punishment, but the righteous into eternal life* (Matthew 25:46).

In flaming fire taking vengeance on those who do not know God, and on those who do not obey the gospel of our Lord Jesus Christ. These shall be punished with everlasting destruction from the presence of the Lord and from the glory of His power (2 Thessalonians 1:8-9).

IT'S JUST A MATTER OF TIME

So it's no secret that I'm a musician, and musicians know about "time signatures." Every piece of music has a time signature that determines how the music is played. When we begin to really live life every day, celebrating the victories, rejoicing in the grace of God, learning how to be of good cheer and even counting it all joy by faith when it's not in the natural, we start living life in a different time signature.

What if God has a time signature for us that is of the Spirit of God instead of the time signature of the world's ways of fast and furious—a frenzy style that often leaves us empty and burned out? What if God has a tempo within His time signature that slows us down enough to actually value relationships and allow the presence of God to be experienced one on one in the day to day and not just from the platform from event to event? What if I can actually learn to live life in His time signature? What are the rhythms of grace?

> *So teach us to number our days, that we may gain a heart of wisdom* (Psalm 90:12).
> *Give us **day by day** our **daily** bread* (Luke 11:3).

There is something about life that is so daily. Life doesn't happen in one moment—life happens one day at a time. I have heard it said that life is not measured by the number of breaths we take, but by the moments that take our breath away. I know it's a bit of a cliché, but it's so true!

I know God is the Giver of my life and my breath, but in terms of my heart God truly does take my breath away! I have been and still am so amazed, so astonished, so in awe of God and how He does this thing called life for us one practical day at a time.

> *This I recall to my mind, therefore I have hope.* ***Through the Lord's mercies we are not consumed, because His compassions fail not. They are new every morning;*** *great is Your faithfulness. "The Lord is my portion," says my soul, "therefore I hope in Him!"* (Lamentations 3:21-24)
>
> *Jesus Christ is the same yesterday, today, and forever* (Hebrews 13:8).
>
> *Blessed be the Lord, who **daily** loads us with benefits, the God of our salvation!* (Psalm 68:19)
>
> *Sing to the Lord, bless His name; proclaim the good news of His salvation from **day to day*** (Psalm 96:2).

> **From the rising of the sun to its going down** *the Lord's name is to be praised* (Psalm 113:3).
> **Every day** *I will bless You, and I will praise Your name forever and ever* (Psalm 145:2).

God created time for *us*, so He obviously knew we would be living this life one breath at a time—second to second, minute by minute, one day at a time. So He also knew that eternal life would start for us in time, not before time and not just after we physically die. We are *in time*, so we need to be *on time* by being present in the moment, listening to what the Holy Spirit is saying, and being available. Live to give!

If you have been walking with God for a while, think back for a minute to when it started. It was just a matter of time before you found out how much God loved you. When you did, you wanted to not only give your heart in response to His love and grace to you, but you want to give your time now into whatever is important to His heart. In a day, you went from living life in one kingdom to another Kingdom, which was brand new to you, even though it was already there waiting for you. If life can't happen on a daily basis, then it won't happen on a weekly, monthly, or yearly basis!

Life *is* about the destination, contrary to what some people teach—because the destination is eternal life in heaven with Jesus. However, because eternal life begins with our beginning, *how* we live needs to become even more important, not just how long we live. The quality of our life here on the earth is a big deal to the heart of God, and it needs to be a big deal to us! We need to break through the toxic limiting ways of the world and live transformed! We need to be in it but not of it.

> *These things I have spoken to you, that **in Me** you may have peace. In the world you will have tribulation; but be of good cheer, I have overcome the world* (John 16:33).

The Greek meaning for "tribulation" is stress, pressure, trouble—but as worshipers we can be of good cheer during this reality. Jesus' life in us is greater than he that is in the world, and in the midst of our stuff, by the grace of God, we can have peace. Jesus gave to us His overcoming-the-world ability and His life in us is greater than the pressure that comes against us.

We don't have to deny reality when things aren't going well in order to live this Spirit-filled life! But on the other hand, we are not going to let our reality take a higher place in our heart than the Word of God. We identify with His Word and believe His report because it is the truth. The truth always trumps reality!

Jesus came to give us abundant life—which is not about us dreading every morning we get up with no purpose or direction. Life is not what we do while waiting to die! God created every day for us to rejoice and be glad in Him, regardless of our circumstances. Life is a journey, and God wants us to do whatever we do to His glory. That process of being and doing happens every day!

I believe we often miss the supernatural life of God in the small moments of our day because we are looking for something spectacular instead. What if we changed our perspective? Our God of wonders deeply loves us. Miracles are everywhere if we acknowledge Him in all our ways instead of being so self-absorbed; His love for us is the greatest miracle of all. God has always wanted an intimate relationship with us. Don't miss the moment! Make memories in the land of promise instead of living in the land of regret, wishing we could finally get into the big time, whatever that means. Don't wait for the big time. The big is in the small! The harvest is always in the seed!

Some dear friends of mine who are in a traveling music ministry were telling me about a conversation they had with a well-meaning lady who came up to them after an evening of worship and ministry and said to them, "Oh, it must be so awesome to be in the big time!" One of the team said to her, "Oh honey, anywhere you are is the big time if you are in the will of God." Start now, start today!

> *Therefore He says: "**Awake**, you who sleep, **arise** from the dead, and Christ will give you light." See then that you walk circumspectly, not as fools but as wise, **redeeming the time**, because the days are evil. Therefore do not be unwise, but understand what the will of the Lord is (Ephesians 5:14-17).*

6

IT'S NOT COMPLICATED

God had a plan that was so important to Him that it had been hidden and protected for ages and generations. He had kept it secret for centuries in order to reveal it in the fullness of time—or in other words, at *exactly the right time.* Guess what? We are living in the time of the revealed plan. The mystery has been revealed, so why don't we get it? Why is the mystery still a mystery to so many?

Colossians 1:26-27 tells us, *"The mystery which has been hidden from ages and from generations, but now has been revealed to His saints. To them God willed to make known what are the riches of the glory of this mystery among the Gentiles: which is Christ in you, the hope of glory."*

The mystery is Christ in us!

Many believers don't really understand this mystery of Christ in us, let alone any hope of glory. *"Christ in you, the hope of glory"* sounds good, but what is it? It's a fair question, yes?

The glory of God is something tangible; it is something that you can see; glory is visible!

As you study glory in Scripture, it has magnificence, splendor, majesty, and greatness in its meaning, according to the dictionary and according to the original languages of both the Hebrew and the Greek. The glory *of* God refers to God's presence that is revealed, manifested, and seen.

This is different from us giving glory *to* God. Giving glory to God is always a response to the glory *of* Christ in us.

The glory of God is tangible because of the presence of God. It is never because of us. It's not our glory! But it is about the glory that is in us. It is always from the Spirit into the physical. It is always from the inside out. It is about the glory of who is in us and looking for a way to shine through us! The life in Christ in us is way bigger and much greater than we think. The apostle Paul writes about this in his second letter to the believers in Corinth:

> *But if the ministry of death, written and engraved on stones, was glorious, so that the children of Israel could not look steadily at the face of Moses because of the glory of his countenance,* **which glory was passing away, how will the ministry of the Spirit not be more glorious?** *For if the ministry of condemnation had glory,* **the ministry of righteousness exceeds much more in glory.** *For even what was made glorious had no glory*

*in this respect, **because of the glory that excels.** For if what is passing away was glorious, **what remains is much more glorious.***

*Therefore, since we have such hope, **we have great boldness of speech**—unlike Moses, who put a veil over his face so that the children of Israel could not look steadily **at the end of what was passing away.** But their minds were blinded. For until this day the same veil remains unlifted in the reading of the Old Testament, because the veil is taken away in Christ. But even to this day, when Moses is read, a veil lies on their heart. Nevertheless, when one turns to the Lord, the veil is taken away. Now the Lord is the Spirit; and where the Spirit of the Lord is, there is liberty. **But we all, with unveiled face, beholding as in a mirror the glory of the Lord, are being transformed into the same image from glory to glory, just as by the Spirit of the Lord*** (2 Corinthians 3:7-18).

Isn't it amazing that the glory of God in us contains riches? Literally, it contains unlimited resources that cause us to be able to live our lives on the earth, transformed by the Spirit of God, and continue being transformed from glory to glory while filled with the presence of God. How is it possible to live like that when encountering real-life situations? This becomes the immediate question, doesn't it?

Again, the Bible tells us that in this life we will have trouble or tribulation. However, Jesus Himself also told us to be of good cheer because of His overcoming life that is now our life. What if we lived life daily from glory to glory instead of from battle to battle? How would life change for us? His presence was always in the temple or the tabernacle, and now your body is God's temple.

We were designed by God to connect. I read a study recently about having significant, meaningful relationships in life with people we know who have our backs in times of trouble. However, we may not have regular contact with them. Then there are "secondary type relationships" most of us have—people we have regular contact with like our neighbor walking the dog, people we say hello to, and the people we know at the places where we shop, work, etc. The study showed that these secondary type relationships actually cause us to live longer than anyone else, because there is connection on a regular basis.

I found the study very interesting because God designed us for relationship starting with Himself first, discovering how much He loves us, and then developing all of our other relationships as a result. It's like the Bible says to seek first the kingdom of God and His righteousness and then all the other things are added. It really is the gift of perspective! We were designed for connection.

As a worshiper, exercising godliness is a big deal! Not only to us but to all the people we come in contact with every day. What kind of effort are you putting into your relationship with God? What about with others? Exercise involves effort, and while we can't ignore the need for physical exercise, neither can we ignore exercise in perfecting godliness in our lives. They both matter. Exercising godliness affects every part of our lives. If we could put a percentage on it, I'd say 80 percent for godliness and 20 percent for physical. Because our body is the temple of God on earth, it's a big deal that we exercise in both areas!

Jesus made it clear that He would have to leave the earth and that sending the Holy Spirit would be better for us. Then He confirmed it by sending Him, the Spirit of God, the Holy Spirit; on the day of Pentecost it happened, which was the beginning of the church. As a result, His presence, the presence of God is available to each of us, not just those who were alive living in Jerusalem at the time.

Sometime during my early years of music ministry, I was taught that the Holy Spirit was very fragile. The image used to describe how fragile He is was that of a dove, as when Jesus was water baptized and the Spirit of God descended upon Him "like a dove."

I had been taught about how easily offended He could be, like a dove we could scare off. I was always so worried that I would somehow sabotage our chances to see Him move in our midst because of something I would do wrong, as in playing the wrong song or a wrong chord in the song. I wondered when would we finally do everything just right so that He could show up and be welcomed in our midst. All the emphasis was placed on what we were not doing right.

I thought it was almost impossible to have access to the Holy Spirit from day to day. I didn't yet know that being a true worshiper meant having a relationship with God in spirit and truth, which is way more than a chord, song, or event!

I seriously thought that we should be very careful even in a public service lest we do something that would cause the

Holy Spirit to leave us—as in, going to the restroom during service, chewing gum, or making too much noise unwrapping my breath mint. God forbid if a baby cried out loud during worship! Everything had to be just right.

I thought that as a worship leader, if our music was in the right key, if we were singing just the right lyrics in the right way, then what *we did* would actually cause the Holy Spirit to show up. If we continued to do everything just right, He might even stay for a visitation—if we were really fortunate! I didn't realize at the time that those things mattered way more to us and disturbed us way more than they ever would matter to God. I was making it much more complicated than it really was.

Unfortunately, "personal preference" was communicated and modeled as the "Spirit's presence."

In the mid-80s while I was living in Tulsa, I was the worship leader at a large church. One day I heard about a lady who was supposedly powerfully manifesting the presence of God. One night she was ministering on the Oral Roberts campus at an independent event, and we heard that she actually began to manifest feathers! We also heard she had been manifesting oil from her own body, which was supposed to be the anointing; even blood from her hands and her head, which was supposed to be the blood of Jesus. This was simply the enemy counterfeiting what Jesus had already done on our behalf. She was so desperate to keep doing something spectacular that she had completely missed the Spirit of God.

The woman had taken actual feathers and stuffed them up her long dress sleeves with elastic cuffs and would reach in and pull some out, with a big wave action, while her hands were lifted in the air and everyone was "worshiping."

One of the cameramen was a friend of mine, and he knew something was very wrong. When he slowed the camera action down, it was clearly seen how she reached into her sleeve to "manifest" the Holy Spirit of God. My friend was used to help expose that fraudulent behavior; she was exposed and her act was over.

When a friend who had his doctorate in ministry heard what had happened, he said, "So what I want to know is, who shot the Holy Ghost?" Wow! It was one of those moments that I laughed so hard I cried. The Holy Ghost is not a dove or a bird of any kind, for that matter! He's also not an it! He is God! The Holy Spirit is just as much God as Jesus and the Father. They are Three in One!

When we teach human doctrines as if they were the Word of God, we are creating a little religious leaven to leaven everything! We pollute the sacred and end up with form and no power. I have to admit I have often found myself feeling sorry for the Spirit of God. I know He's big enough to take care of Himself, but I'm just telling you, I know His heart for us is to experience so much more!

I was always worried about offending God and messing up to where He would eventually just leave me like the tabernacle stolen by the Philistines in the Old Covenant! What I discovered later is that we can't offend God now, even though, sadly, there are many offensive things everywhere in our world today. We can't offend God because God is love and love doesn't take offense. When Jesus fully paid the price on the cross for everything offensive and vile, everything sinful and broken, everything sick and diseased in Himself, the offense and all the requirement of the law was nailed to that cross. Jesus paid it all! God's love is greater than offense. It's not complicated!

Colossians 2:13-15 tells us, *"He has…forgiven you all trespasses, having wiped out the handwriting of requirements that was against us, which was contrary to us. And He has taken it out of the way, having nailed it to the cross. Having disarmed principalities and powers, He made a public spectacle of them, triumphing over them in it."*

However, *we can grieve* the Spirit of God today according to the Word of God. This is amazing to think about because it shows us the Spirit of God has Spirit feelings. Did you know it's possible to grieve the Spirit of God? He is passionate, in fact, even jealous over us being conformed to the image of Christ and not conformed to the ways of the world. That is so amazing!

> *And do not grieve the Holy Spirit of God, by whom you were sealed for the day of redemption* (Ephesians 4:30).

So how do we grieve God, you ask? We grieve Him by living with a stolen identity. If we choose to live carnally, instead of identified with Christ, it grieves the Holy Spirit. He has so identified with us because we identified with Christ in His death, burial, and resurrection. Wow!

Ephesians 4:29 of that same passage tells us that when we let unwholesome talk come out of our mouths instead of bringing grace to those who listen, it grieves the Holy Spirit.

When we live with bitterness, rage, anger, and participate in evil speaking and loud quarreling, all these things grieve the Holy Spirit because He has so much more for us to the exclusion of those behaviors. Again, I'm amazed that when we cause Him to grieve, He remains with us.

The Holy Spirit can also be quenched; did you know that? *"Do not quench the Spirit"* (1 Thessalonians 5:19). So what does that mean exactly? We could say it like this: Do not suppress, stifle, or extinguish the Spirit. Do not try to eliminate His divine influence. Quenching the Spirit means we can limit Him by ignoring Him in our life and in our relationships, let alone in our gatherings. To respond with "a quench" is to not respond! Let me ask you, does *"Do not* quench the Spirit" sound like a suggestion to you?

You can also frustrate the grace of God in your life. Frustrating the grace of God is the last area I want to highlight and that we need to understand. We can't offend God now thanks to Jesus, but we can grieve Him. And now, I'm telling you that we can frustrate His grace? How on earth do we frustrate the grace of God?

> *I do not frustrate the grace of God: for if righteousness come by the law, then Christ is dead in vain* (Galatians 2:21 KJV).

The New King James says it this way:

> *I do not set aside the grace of God; for if righteousness comes through the law, then Christ died in vain* (Galatians 2:21).

Other Bible versions use the words nullify, ignore, reject, turn my back, cast away the grace of God. Any time we put ourselves or someone else back under the Old Covenant, we frustrate the grace of God, setting aside the very provision that God made available for us to live in the power of His presence. We aren't justified and made righteous by the works of the law, because we've been crucified with Christ. I'm living life now with my body as His temple, living by faith in the Son of God who loved me and gave Himself for me—for you. I realize now that it's only because of grace that I can receive by faith!

Think about how many times we have frustrated the grace of God in our worship gatherings.

Years ago, I was imagining what that perfect public worship service would look like and sound like. I imagined how the Spirit of God would roll in like a cloud or a fog—kind of like what happened at the dedication of the temple of Solomon, where the presence of God was so strong the priests couldn't even stand. They weren't even asking for the presence to fall! I was so upset with God, because they had such a manifestation of the presence of God. We were the ones who were supposed to be under a better covenant with better promises. We were supposed to be seeing the greater, not the lesser. We were even asking for the presence of God to fall on us!

Where was our move of God? Where was our manifestation of the Presence so strong that we couldn't even stand up? I was mad! I had tried so hard to do the right things, just like I had with my early morning prayer times. It just never seemed to be quite enough for some reason. The harder I tried, the more frustrated I became until I just wanted to quit! I was trying so hard to love God with my whole heart. What I didn't yet know was what a difference it would make when I realized God loved me first with His whole heart, which allowed me to respond. I wasn't initiating anything!

One day I contemplated quitting out of sheer frustration and exhaustion. Then it was as if the Holy Spirit said to me, "Daniel, wake up! Don't you even realize yet that you are living under a better covenant with better promises? Didn't I tell you that Christ is already in you as the hope of glory!"

Being a New Covenant believer with Christ alive in me as the hope of glory, why would I still think that the glory needed to come from outer space somewhere? Why would I put myself under something already fulfilled? It's not complicated. I was looking in all the wrong places.

While Jesus was still on the earth physically, He said in John 14:16-17:

> *And I will pray the Father, and He will give you another Helper, that He may abide with you for-ever—the Spirit of truth, whom the world cannot receive, because it neither sees Him nor knows Him; but you know Him, for **He dwells with you and will be in you.***

The difference between *with* you and *in* you is huge. It's not complicated! Why don't we get it? Even still, it's so amazing to me that the glory, that anointing, the very presence of God, that fullness of God is made available through the life of Christ to every believer.

We know that the Spirit of God makes the Word of God real to us, and He did just that for me that day! He revealed His Word to me. I am forever grateful! Let's look at the verse again:

> *To them God willed to make known what are the riches of the glory of this mystery among the Gentiles: which is Christ in you, the hope of glory* (Colossians 1:27).

Wow, I was so overcome with gratitude that my eyes just started leaking! I began to realize that the Holy Spirit, the very Spirit of God whom Jesus described as another Comforter like Himself, was not the fragile, easily offended Spirit at all. Nor was He the Victorian English gentleman type of Spirit of God I had developed in my mind!

I learned that the Holy Spirit was strong and powerful. He was going to do life with us on a daily basis and be our Helper in the day-to-day nitty-gritty—in fact, even in the messy places of life. There was nothing fragile about Him at all.

I was leading worship in a church in Southern California in the early '90s when one morning our guest speaker brought very stern correction to a young nine-year-old boy who got up to use the restroom while he was preaching. The preacher got red in the face and yelled for the boy to sit down. He said that because the boy got up from his seat, he had ruined the anointing that was there, causing the Spirit of God to leave. Seriously?!

I was so surprised and shocked that I could hardly think. I was stunned! *Did this really just happen?* Talk about legalism and Old Covenant thinking! I have often wondered what happened to that boy's heart afterward and what he is doing today as a man. Hopefully it didn't derail him or cause irreparable damage in his life.

I remember thinking, *If the anointing really is this fragile, then we are in big trouble!* Then I thought, *Maybe that's why we are in big trouble—because of the way we have thought about the presence of God.* The Bible says the Holy Spirit would never leave or forsake us. What was happening? How are we ever going to reach this generation with the good news of the gospel if the Holy Spirit is that troubled by a child going to the restroom?

A BIG LIE ABOUT THE HOLY SPIRIT

One of the biggest lies so many people believe about the Holy Spirit is that He is a gentleman. People mean well, and we know what they generally mean when they say that. However, the Bible never says that about Him! The word *gentleman*, according to the Merriam-Webster Dictionary, "is a man who treats other people in a proper or polite way." While that is very noble, the problem with this concept being applied to the Holy Spirit is we reduce Him to our definition of whatever we think "proper and polite" is. Every culture and every generation has a different set of standards to apply to that definition. To make it even worse, we think that living proper and polite is godly. Sadly, we often think today that *nice* is one of the fruit of the Spirit of God. *It's not!* (Hang on, I'll explain!)

I believe much of the church today has slipped into a "doctrine of devils" that has reduced us to being compliant, politically correct, tolerant, and polite according to the current tide of culture. This thinking has turned many of our gatherings into form without power as a result. We want everyone to be "okay."

The apostle Paul told young Timothy to run from this kind of thinking. Form without power is just a rut, and it's been said that a rut is a grave with the ends open. So don't get stuck in a rut!

Having a form of godliness but denying its power. And from such people turn away! (2 Timothy 3:5)

Jesus says in John 14:26: *"But the Helper, the Holy Spirit, whom the Father will send in My name, He will teach you all things, and bring to your remembrance all things that I said to you."*

The Holy Spirit is "the Comforter" so that you get out of your comfort zone!

The Holy Spirit will always remain the Comforter, but don't be falsely led into thinking your personal physical comfort is what is on God's heart! Don't misunderstand—God is not out to make you miserable or frustrated. He loves to help you at all times, including helping in times of distress! However, He is building the church, and the gates of hell will not prevail!

Jesus gave us authority in His name to do what needs to be done. He is going to build through us because we are the church. He wants us to use what has been provided in Christ and partner with Him by the Holy Spirit so that He can help us make that happen in the earth today. Building the church means He is building you and me because we are the church. Trust me when I say He is going to lead us into situations and circumstances that will not always be comfortable. God, however, will always be the *"the Father of mercies and God of all comfort,"* according to 2 Corinthians 1:3.

Is the gospel about His Kingdom or my comfort? Let me give you a worship example. Sadly, some people think today that worship is about whatever is comfortable for them. I have even heard many leaders say to the people something like they should worship in whatever way is comfortable, even though Jesus never even hinted at anything like that! Did you ever hear Jesus telling the disciples just to do whatever was comfortable for them? Wow, really? No.

Jesus said our model was spirit and truth, not what is comfortable! True worshipers *must* worship in spirit and truth.

I will never forget the first time I raised my hands in worship! It was very uncomfortable! Lifting hands in worship is very scriptural. I was obviously led by the Holy Spirit to do it, because the Holy Spirit will always agree with the Word of God, but He is not required to agree with what we think or what is comfortable to us at the time. It was uncomfortable at first, but I discovered that it works much better when we agree with Him instead of what we think is comfortable at the time. It takes time, and it's just a matter of time.

As disciples, we need to seek first the Kingdom, not comfort! Unbelievers think that the things of the Spirit of God are foolishness:

> *But the natural man does not receive the things of the Spirit of God, for they are foolishness to him; nor can he know them, because they are spiritually discerned* (1 Corinthians 2:14).

Why are we trying to make God in our image instead of realizing that we are made in His?

Remember, even unbelievers worship; they just don't worship God! Being a true worshiper means you're a believer who has an authentic relationship of spirit and truth, which is what makes you a true worshiper. It's not complicated, but sometimes it is uncomfortable!

My wife and I were in a very uncomfortable situation a few years back that involved a family member. As we were walking in love in the situation with our discomfort, we heard the Holy Spirit minister this to our hearts: "Your comfort is nothing compared to their eternity!" Just one word, just one Holy Spirit moment will change everything! What is the Holy Spirit hearing Jesus say?

Please read this next verse slowly and thoughtfully:

> *Who **comforts us in all our tribulation**, that we may be able to comfort those who are in any trouble, with the comfort with which we ourselves are comforted by God* (2 Corinthians 1:4).

There is a big difference in being comforted by the Comforter and being comfortable. Paul and Silas were not comfortable after being beaten (Acts 16), but they were comforted by the Wonderful Counselor to the point that they sang songs of praise at midnight! Then they brought supernatural comfort and joy to many others as a result and eventually deliverance from bondage!

> *For our light affliction, which is but for a moment, is working for us a far more exceeding and eternal weight of glory* (2 Corinthians 4:17).

If Jesus had been personally more about comfort than confronting, can you imagine how different the Gospels would be today? What would the encounters with the demoniac, the money changers in the temple, the stone throwers (those who didn't cast the first stone) actually look like? I can guarantee you that "the Word who always was" would never have left His comfort in heaven to be born in a stable and become "the Word made flesh." Talk about messy places! The Holy Spirit should have known better than to deal with messy people, right? *Wrong!*

The *daily* of life presents all kinds of situations that require you to depend on the Spirit of God within you—instead of depending on you. I remember, growing up, singing an old hymn with the lyrics: "I need Thee every hour." I have found that to be absolutely correct!

If comfortable was the goal, Jesus would never have spent forty days fasting and, as a very hungry Man, resisted temptation from the devil not once but three times, declaring, "It is written." Each time Jesus showed us how to resist the enemy by speaking the Word of God from our hearts! If comfortable was the goal, He would certainly never have taken thirty-nine stripes on His body so you could be healed in yours or have gone to the cross on your behalf by becoming sin. Jesus didn't do the will of God because it was convenient! It wasn't about His comfort, but He intimately knew the true Comforter, the Spirit of God!

Jesus gave us power and authority to work the works of God. Yet in much of the church today, we've taken the fruit of the Spirit and the gifts of the Spirit and reduced the ministry that Jesus paid in full for us to have into a modern-day tolerant image of *nice!* Being PC doesn't mean Powerful through Christ, now does it? PC is nothing but being politically correct. It stinks! *Nice* is not a fruit of the Spirit; love is, gentleness is, kindness is, and so forth.

God's love is never rude, but it sure is bold! Love is not always nice, but love is our motivation for healing the sick and driving out demons and doing the same works that Jesus did— just like He told us to do. The love of God always loves, and love speaks the truth in love. Love is kind. The love of God is always expressed as compassion in meeting people's needs.

When a situation calls for it, seeing people delivered is kind. It is a perfect demonstration of how we need to always function in compassion and boldness at the same time. Love listens carefully and love spends quality time. Love doesn't always remain silent, and it doesn't always say what is politically correct or even socially acceptable. Love speaks the truth! When truth is spoken, it is spoken in love.

Do you remember when WWJD was popular in Christian culture in the 1990s? It stood for What Would Jesus Do. It was a reminder of our belief that we were to demonstrate the life of Christ at all times. What would Jesus do? What would you do? We are to show forth His salvation, not hide it.

The modern-day church belief that the Holy Spirit is a "gentleman" and will never do something to make you uncomfortable is a lie! He will lead you into all truth and show you things to come. It won't always be comfortable, but it will always be good! Just like God is always good, but good is not always God. So it is also with the Holy Spirit always being the Comforter, but not the One always making you comfortable!

Come on, it's time to "Come alive!" It's time to stand up and shout out the truth from the rooftops that you are hearing in your quiet place of prayer, worship, Bible study, and intimacy with the Spirit of God. Again, remember the Spirit of God wrote the Word of God, so hearing God will agree with the Word of God. The Word is the truth, so we never have to wonder if what we are hearing is accurate. What does the Word say?

Don't be a spiritual wimp thinking that the Holy Spirit is some wimpy God figure. Be bold! Feed the five thousand *and* challenge those who want to "cast the first stone"! Bless the little children *and* turn over the tables of the money changers! Cast your nets on the other side *and* cast out devils!

After Jesus ascended to heaven, look at what the Word says about when the Holy Spirit was first given out in a big way, not just to one person for an assignment:

But you shall receive power when the Holy Spirit has come upon you; and you shall be witnesses to Me in Jerusalem, and in all Judea and Samaria and to the end of the earth (Acts 1:8).

The Holy Spirit never manipulates us or forces His way against our will. I believe this is where people often get the false idea of Him being a gentleman. We have to be careful assigning a name to Him that the Bible doesn't use to describe Him; otherwise, we will come up with something that may seem right but is not. We don't want to create another idol! The Holy Spirit is love, and all the fruit of His love is the fruit of the Spirit. However, not one of those nine fruit is "gentlemanly."

Think carefully about what you're reading because the Holy Spirit is not rude and He is not weird (selah!), but God's ways are higher than ours and that is why we have to renew our mind to how *He* thinks and how *He* does life!

God loves people and is not intimidated by sinful, messy, broken people. Nor is He threatened by people living with a stolen identity like the woman at the well or the woman caught in adultery, or, or, or…! God's love intimates, never intimidates!

If you want to know what the Holy Spirit's love is like all you have to do is read chapter 13 of 1 Corinthians to see His kind of love. The Holy Spirit is God and God is love! He is just as much God as the Father and the Son. They are not three separate Gods, but rather three in One! What was the Father like? Jesus came to show us the Father! (See John 14:8.)

The Holy Spirit will meet us where we are. We must learn to cooperate with Him and partner with Him because God is God! God is all powerful and He is still the Great I AM! We can never reduce God to our image or think we have Him all figured out. Every day our expectation needs to be in the power of God and not in our own wisdom (1 Corinthians 2:4-5).

However, He is our Helper and He really does want to be involved in our lives, helping us—even helping us get out of our comfort zones. What if it's time to step out of the boat? What if it's time to do something different?

Remember how I said that the Gospels are the transitional period between the Old Covenant and the Beginning of the church age? Well, look at what Jesus said in the Gospel of John about something that would happen then in part, but have fulfillment during the church age:

> *And I will pray the Father, and He will give you another Helper, that He may abide with you forever—the Spirit of truth, whom the world cannot receive, because it neither sees Him nor knows Him; but you know Him, for He dwells with you and will be in you* (John 14:16-17).

Let's not reduce God to our modern-day television image of Mr. Nice Guy!

Our God is an awesome God who is the Mighty One in the midst of us both personally and publicly in our gatherings. What if we really believed that we are the place of His presence?

Acts 7:47-48 says, *"But Solomon built Him a house. However, the Most High does not dwell in temples made with hands."*

Hopefully by now you know that we are the temple of God. Hopefully it's not complicated anymore. In the ancient world, until the birth of the church, any thought of the presence of God living in us was a total mystery. But now we can know it by reading confirmations in the New Covenant. Life isn't complicated; knowing that God loves you, everything falls into place—the place of His presence.

Most people live very carnal lives, meaning we live by our five physical senses; consequently, we are always looking on the outward appearance for confirmation, for identity, and even for comparison to see if we are good enough or if we measure up. God, on the other hand, looks at our hearts. So here's the deal—God clearly knows that your whole life will flow through your heart, which is why your heart matters.

7

YOUR HEART MATTERS

For the Lord does not see as man sees; for man looks at the outward appearance, but the Lord looks at the heart (1 Samuel 16:7).

One day a lawyer who was also Pharisee asked Jesus a question, testing Him. What did he ask?

> *"Teacher, which is the great commandment in the law?" Jesus said to him, "You shall love the Lord your God with all your **heart**, with all your **soul**, and with all your **mind**.' This is the first and great commandment. And the second is like it: 'You shall **love** your neighbor as yourself.' On these two commandments hang all the Law and the Prophets"* (Matthew 22:36-40).

The ancient prophet Ezekiel prophesied about a time coming when something so new was going to happen that even the prophet didn't fully understand what he was saying; as I have clearly shown you, they didn't have context to know that we as New Covenant believers were going to be the place of God's presence—the very temple of God in the earth, with the very presence of God living inside of us!

It would be like trying to imagine smartphones or the internet in the 1950s. God was letting them know something big and something new was coming that would require change and produce transformation.

Ezekiel 36:26 says, *"I will give you a new heart and put a new spirit within you; I will take the heart of stone out of your flesh and give you a heart of flesh."*

Then almost toward the end of the New Testament, we discover an interesting warning about the heart:

> *Beware, brethren, lest there be in any of you an **evil heart of unbelief** in departing from the living God; but exhort one another daily, while it is called "Today," **lest any of you be hardened through the deceitfulness of sin** (Hebrews 3:12-13).*

Psalm 95:8 tells us, *"Do not harden your hearts."* So, obviously, it is possible to do so. And Proverbs 4:23 says, *"Keep your heart with all diligence, for out of it spring the issues of life."* The New International Version says it this way: *"Above all else, guard your heart, for everything you do flows from it."* Notice *we* are the ones who have to keep it, guard it.

Your heart matters to God and needs to matter to you, because everything you do flows from your heart; 100 percent of the issues of life spring into existence from your heart. Your heart is very valuable, and you have to choose what gets written on your heart, which is why it's under constant attack. The enemy hates you and wants to steal, kill, and destroy you! He wants you to have an overloaded heart, be stressed out all the time, and worse, have a heart that becomes hardened or what the Bible refers to as a stony heart.

In this chapter, we will unpack this topic of the heart, as well as the important revelation of spirit, soul, and body and how it relates to the heart, because it matters. No, it *really* matters! You cannot worship inside out without this revelation.

> Life happens, but what we do with what happens becomes the heart of the matter!

Let me give you a couple of examples. When you start to self-protect, for instance, you develop a dysfunctional hiding place that will eventually isolate you and keep you lonely and miserable. In trying to self-protect, you will build a tower around your heart that will isolate you, not protect you. Inner vows often accompany a hardened or stony heart. They often happen early in life from learned behaviors—you know, disappointments, rejections, disillusions—which then serve as directives that keep us hidden, sometimes for years!

As adults, when it seems we are not receiving from God, it is usually because of a hardened heart of unbelief. Even if you don't want to be like that, how can you change what's happening inside?

If you're a believer but you have allowed your heart to develop into a *"sinful, unbelieving heart,"* it doesn't mean you are an evil person or that your spirit needs to get born again, again! Rather, what you are allowing to happen in your soul is what is predominately poisoning your heart. Before you despair, the good news is you can do something about it with the help of the Holy Spirit and the Word of God! Remember, spirit and truth is the only way to worship! It is what keeps us balanced.

I clearly remember years ago being *so* excited discovering that I am a three-part being—spirit, soul, and body—and how much that helped me in my relationship with God. Being a worshiper took on new meaning for me as I began to connect Scriptures that previously didn't make sense to me, including 1 Thessalonians 5:23: *"Now may the God of peace Himself sanctify* [set you apart] *you completely; and may your whole spirit, soul, and body be preserved blameless at the coming of our Lord Jesus Christ."*

Soon after that, however, a problem developed when I heard various teachers minister on the heart. I couldn't quite figure out where this idea of the heart fit in the mix of spirit, soul, and body.

I remember one day back in the early '80s when I was studying this. I had been so focused on this for quite some time in my home office. Finally, I went downstairs to the kitchen where my wife was preparing a lovely dinner, and right in the middle of her preparations I tried to begin this deep theological discussion on the preparations of the heart and what was on my heart at the time.

So I asked my wife, "Where do you think the heart is, honey? I mean this is really critical for us to know. You know, your spiritual heart. Where do you think it is in us?"

She gave me that look. Uh huh, you know the look—the one that only a wife can give her husband, as she was up to her elbows in dinner preparations. She said, "Daniel, really? I don't think it really matters as long as you just *use* it. So why don't you just use yours right now and set the table for me!"

We both laughed, but the truth was it mattered to both of us. What I've learned in talking to many people about this is it seems to be a common question. Several people have said, "Okay, I get the spirit, soul, and body thing, but now I'm messed up with the concept of the heart." What people now tell me was what I had experienced as well.

When teachers taught about the heart, they talked about it being in the inward parts of our belly. I remember thinking, *What does that mean?* I even looked up the Greek word and it said it is belly, womb, and innermost being. I remember thinking, *So if it's near the physical belly, is it near the spleen or closer to your liver or what?* Many were without understanding, especially me! I would find verses like the following:

> *So He* [Jesus] *said to them* [the disciples], *"**Are you thus without understanding** also? Do you not perceive that whatever enters a man from outside cannot defile him, because it **does not enter his heart but his***

*stomach, and is eliminated, thus purifying all foods?"
And He said, "What comes **out** of a man, **that** defiles a
man. **For from within, out of the heart** of men, **pro-
ceed evil thoughts**, adulteries, fornications, murders,
thefts, covetousness, wickedness, deceit, lewdness, an
evil eye, blasphemy, pride, foolishness and these evil
things come from within and defile a man"* (Mark
7:18-23).

What? I always believed that our thoughts came from our
mind, but this Scripture passage in Mark says they come from
our hearts. Which is it?

I also found Proverbs 20:27 which says. *"The spirit of a man
is the lamp of the Lord, searching all the inner depths of his heart."*

I would hear teachers teach about the importance of getting
the Word of God from your head into your heart. Then I was
really confused! I thought I was supposed to renew my mind—
according to Romans 12:1-2—but now they were telling me
that it wasn't near as good as getting it down into my heart.
Where was that? How did that relate to my spirit or my soul?

If I was a three-part being as I had been taught, then where
did the heart fit into this mix?

Many people taught me early on that the spirit was the
heart. They taught that the heart and the human spirit were
the same thing. That's what I had believed for years.

However, now things were getting more confused instead
of less! Mark 7:21 made no sense then, because if my spirit was
my heart and my spirit was born again, then how could it have

evil or sinful thoughts? How can my heart have thoughts at all? I thought my mind had thoughts!

Jesus says in Matthew 12:34 that out of the abundance of the heart our mouth speaks. And it says in James 3:10 that out of the same mouth proceeds blessing and cursing and that these things should not be so. Then James goes on to ask the same question I was asking: *"Does a spring send forth fresh water and bitter from the same opening?"* (James 3:11).

If evil thoughts come from the heart and the heart is spirit, then we have confusion, and where confusion is there is every evil work according to James 3:16. So my born-again spirit has confusion and every evil work? I wanted to throw my hands up, wave a white flag, and just surrender to what seemed to be impossible. It just didn't make sense!

Well, I certainly don't claim to have all the answers on this for sure, but I'm so excited to share with you what the Holy Spirit showed me and what I have learned through this process. It sure helped me and I think it will you too! I'm so thankful that He is the teacher who leads us into all truth!

I began to see that bitter water and sweet water *can* come from the heart but *not* out of the born-again spirit. First Peter 3:4 describes our spirit as the hidden person of the heart:

> *Rather let it be the **hidden person of the heart**, with the incorruptible beauty of a gentle and quiet spirit, which is very precious in the sight of God.*

In not understanding spirit, soul, and body, some have even doubted their own salvation as a result. Unbelief would start to set in because they thought they were going to become a brand-new person instead of a new spirit, which is where the new creation happens.

Our spirit is instantly transformed, but our soul is progressively being changed through the influence of spirit and truth. It is a lifelong process where we are transformed by the renewing of our minds *and* the restoring of our souls by marinating, or meditating, in spirit and truth.

James 1:21 tells us that we need to *"receive with meekness the implanted word, which is able to save your souls."* Hebrews 10:38-39 talks about the *"saving of the soul."* And 3 John 2 says, *"Beloved, I pray that you may prosper in all things and be in health, just as your soul prospers."*

As we look into the New Covenant revelation of being a new creation, we discover that when the Bible speaks of the inner self, it is speaking of the heart or what is referred to as the spirit and the soul.

We are told in 2 Corinthians 4:16: *"Therefore we do not lose heart. Even though our outward man is perishing, yet the inward man is being renewed day by day."* That is a wonderful promise! Take a minute to think about this truth—your inward self is being renewed day by day! That is incredible, isn't it?

As I further studied the words *spirit* and *soul*, there were times when the Bible was using the word *soul* in a general way to mean a person's life or the word *spirit* to mean breath. It became clear that we are three-part beings, as 1 Thessalonians 5:23 declares. Our heart is not just our spirit, but rather our inner self. The spirit and the soul together make up the heart, our inner self.

The word for "spirit" in the Greek is *pneuma,* while the Greek word for "soul" is *psyche,* and the Greek word for "body" is *soma.* Therefore, Scripture clearly shows us a division within humankind as people, but the only thing that can really separate us like this is the Word of God.

Hebrews 4:12 says, *"For the word of God is living and powerful, and sharper than any two-edged sword, piercing even to the division of soul and spirit, and of joints and marrow, and is a discerner of the thoughts and intents of the heart."*

The word here for "division" is the Greek word *merismos,* which literally means to divide or to separate. You can't do this, and neither can psychiatrists or religion! Only the Word of God can divide you from the inside out. The Holy Spirit will always help you to be separated *to* the Word, while the enemy will always try to separate you *from* the Word!

If you stay in the Word long enough, the Word will divide or separate, literally cut off, whatever needs to be separated from you in order for you to live the abundant life that Jesus came to give you. Live it from the inside out! God wants you conformed to the image of Christ in every area of your life.

I want you to think about this—before you were born again, your whole inner self, your heart, was united, but it was lost. You were dead spiritually, but you did have a single heart, a united heart, so to speak. Your spirit was dead, but your soul was in charge and did whatever it wanted to do. Before you were born again, your soul was used to being in control—and it still wants to be in control.

Hebrews 10:22 says, *"Let us draw near with a true heart in full assurance of faith, having our hearts sprinkled from an evil conscience and our bodies washed with pure water."*

God did His part, and now He was expecting me to do mine by responding. I was the one who had to offer myself as a living sacrifice. I was the one who had to offer the sacrifice of praise, the fruit of my lips giving thanks. I was the one who had to draw near, but now, for the first time in my life, I realized it was all happening within my soul. My soul was where I did the drawing near—my will, mind, and emotions all being fueled by the Spirit of God within my human spirit.

A HEART OF THANKSGIVING

David knew the heartful principle of thanksgiving. Even though he didn't have the Spirit of God living in him, he still knew how important it was to remember God's faithfulness and what God had already brought him through.

Psalm 92:1-2 says, *"It is good to give thanks to the Lord, and to sing praises to Your name, O Most High; to declare Your loving-kindness in the morning, and Your faithfulness every night."* It is good. Who is it good for? You! It is very beneficial for you to live in an attitude of gratitude! Even medical professionals will tell you the many health benefits that result from a thankful, positive attitude.

Thanksgiving changes your heart perspective.

What is the first thing you think about when you wake up? Do you have a list of problems and challenges at the top of the pile? It's easy to think about all that is not right. Maybe for you, this is what you think about before you go to bed at night. The list of problems just seems to appear out of nowhere!

By thinking about what you can be thankful for, you can bring every negative *"thought into captivity to the obedience of Christ"* (2 Corinthians 10:5) and make them submit to the finished works of Jesus!

So opening your will with thanksgiving to the realm of the Spirit allows your soul to be Spirit-filled to where you will soon find yourself not only entering the gates, but now coming into God's courts with heartfelt praise. Being heart-happy involves your mind and what you think about. Paul clearly addresses this fact of life:

> **Be anxious for nothing**, *but in everything by prayer and supplication,* **with thanksgiving**, *let your requests be made known to God; and the peace of God, which surpasses all understanding, will* **guard your hearts and minds** *through Christ Jesus. Finally, brethren, whatever things are true, whatever things are noble, whatever things are just, whatever things are pure, whatever things are lovely, whatever things are of good report,* **if there is any virtue and if there is anything praiseworthy—meditate on these things** (Philippians 4:6-8).

As your mind becomes more and more filled with the Spirit of God, your emotions will follow your thoughts. Your soul will become more and more aware of God instead of being stressed out and conformed to the ways of our crazy world!

Instead of your emotions controlling you, your emotions can serve to help you express your heart and help you to enjoy life more abundantly. It is all connected together and needs to be integrated. That only happens when we allow our souls to be filled with the Spirit of God and the Word of God.

Some people have believed a lie for so long they actually think it's the truth. They have become deceived by rejecting the truth in order to believe a lie. The Word is the truth (John 17:17) and you can't be deceived if you know the truth, because God's truth sets you free. But you can reject the truth, choosing to believe what seems real to you, and thus deceive your own heart. Remember, 100 percent of the issues of life flow through the heart!

> *For as he thinks **in his heart,** so is he* (Proverbs 23:7).
> *Therefore whoever hears these sayings of Mine, and does them, I will liken him to a **wise man who built** his house on the rock* (Matthew 7:24).

Notice we need to hear and do.

Mark 3:25 says, *"If a house is divided against itself, that house cannot stand."* Think about us being that house and how we become unstable in all our ways when we are not being built on the Word of God!

TRANSFORMATION

God never planned on our soul being in control! Your soul was not designed to lead. However, our spirit was, while being led by the Spirit of God. That is a huge truth to understand.

In the Garden of Eden, the enemy came to Adam and Eve and first challenged what God had told them by asking, "Did God really say…?" He does the same thing with us today, doesn't he? The enemy told them they would not die—that they would actually be like God. Well, they were already like God—and they did die, spiritually! The enemy told them they could be in charge, they could be independent, they could do life without God. Wrong!

We have the same lie today—not dying is simply reincarnation, and becoming like God is humanism.

The soul in control can never produce spirit! Only the Spirit of God can produce spirit! (See John 3:6 and John 6:63 again for review.) Remember, believers are the true worshipers, and this is why this revelation is critical for us to understand in this generation! Much of our worship today is activated or originated from the soul—using its own will, mind, and emotions—instead of from the spirit within us in response to the Spirit of God.

Many of our gatherings have become us being conformed into the image of the world's way of thinking and doing instead of us being the image of Christ to the world. More than anything, how we think, our perspective, affects the substance of our heart, not just the style of the music or the fashion, which is seriously just about as meaningful as food.

It's not what we take in, Jesus said, it's what comes out from within our hearts. We must worship inside out!

The condition of our heart is literally a matter of life and death!

> *For assuredly, I say to you, whoever says to this moun-tain, "Be removed and be case into the sea," and **does not doubt in his heart**, **but believes** that those things he says will be done, he will have whatever he says* (Mark 11:23).

If your heart is in neutral, overloaded, shut down, or full of unbelief, nothing godly is going to be flowing out from it! Instead of a river, you'll be more like the dead sea! This is why your heart really does matter!

What are you speaking? What are you saying? You will speak whatever is in your heart, so if you want to know what is in your heart in abundance, listen to what you are saying!

YOUR HEART IS VALUED GROUND

> *And He said to them, "Do you not understand this parable? How then will you understand all the par-ables? **The sower sows the word.** And these are the ones by the wayside where the word is sown. When they hear, Satan comes immediately and takes away the word that was sown in their hearts. These like-wise are the ones sown on stony ground who, when they hear the word immediately receive it with glad-ness; and they have no root in themselves, and so*

*endure only for a time. Afterward, **when tribulation or persecution arises** for the word's sake, immediately they stumble. Now these are the ones sown among thorns; they are the ones who hear the word, and the cares of this world, the deceitfulness of riches, and the desires for other things entering in choke the word, and it becomes unfruitful. But **these are the ones sown on good ground, those who hear the word, accept it, and bear fruit: some thirty fold, some sixty, and some a hundred***" (Mark 4:13-20).

Then in Mark 4:28, Jesus speaks something very interesting about the ground. He says, *"For the earth yields crops by itself: first the blade, then the head, after that the full grain in the head."*

Again, we see how the ground is what produces and will grow what is sown into it! Jesus was using a natural reality to speak of the spiritual dynamic of receiving the Word of God into our hearts. The goal of planting is always to experience harvest. Fruitfulness happens when something fruitful is planted. If you're not happy with your harvest, change what you are planting. God's Word is alive and powerful.

There will be revelation—knowledge revealed to us by the Spirit of the Lord, our Teacher—and if we receive it, it leads to transformation that results in manifestation. Then at this point, it's as though you own it. It becomes part of your lifestyle; it's yours and it belongs to you. You can hear someone else's revelation, but at some point it has to become your own. Living off of someone else's revelation only leads to an imitation.

In this same parable, Jesus refers to the soul part of our heart that is in process. What we sow into our soil is what produces a harvest. It is a process that starts with the reborn spirit. We learn to live from this new place by having a relationship based in spirit and truth, learning to bring the soul into submission to the will of God.

Notice that Jesus said *when* tribulation or persecution comes, not *if* it comes. It comes because of the word that was sown in your heart. Not because of what you did wrong or didn't do enough of, like we so often think. The enemy desperately wants to separate you from the Word of God. He loves to beat us up with our old performance-based thinking, *Coulda, shoulda, me, me, me!* Remember, you don't have to make the Word of God come true; it *is* true! You just need to believe and receive it by sowing it into the soil of your heart.

Is our ground hard? Is it stony? Is it full of thorns? Our unbelief doesn't change the Word of God, but it does limit us. The issue is never the Word; the issue is what's going on in the heart! It is the soil condition of your heart, and remember—the issues of life flow from the heart.

This is so big, because honestly this part of the parable I believe is where most people are living on a daily basis. The three biggies: 1) care; 2) deceitfulness of riches, or we could say the love of money; and 3) desire for other things that cause the Word to become unfruitful in us and through us.

Each of these areas could easily be a chapter on their own. But let me briefly share.

THE CARES OF LIFE

The cares of life can be very overwhelming! Life happens! This word for "cares" also means anxieties. Today we would typically refer to it as stress. This is why we are told in 1 Peter 5:7, *"Casting all your care upon Him, for He cares for you."* When we really know that God cares for us and loves us, then we will trust Him and will stop taking the cares and stress of everyday life into our hearts. Instead, we will cast our cares on Him.

What does that even mean? Cast our cares? How do we do that? Aren't we just supposed to stuff it and act like it doesn't exist? No.

The word for "cast" in the Greek language means "to throw upon or to place upon, to throw away." We are not told to ignore the cares of life. But we are not supposed to identify with all that stress trying to tell you how to live. Don't ignore it; cast it onto God!

One day when I was casting my care on the Lord, I said out loud, "Lord, I feel like I'm throwing my garbage on You!" Then He told me the most amazing thing: *"No,* when you do what I've told you to do in My Word, it is praise to Me!" Wow! His response changed me forever! Whenever we are doers of the Word and not hearers only, it pleases the Lord. It gives Him praise!

I was on my way to work and some major things were going on personally causing a lot of stress. I began to sing and make melody in my heart to the Lord and I found myself, saying, *"No!* I don't care! I'm not gonna care, I cast my care, because *You* care!" I started laughing and almost turned it into a rap by adding rhythm to it and repeating it over and over! It was a fun way to have the Holy Spirit help me cast my care on Him that day.

The cares of life include marriage, children, grandchildren, aging loved ones, our health, careers, etc. You get the point. There is *much* to care about. But let me encourage you. Instead of adding one more thing, let's just do the *one thing* that matters, and *do* what Jesus said to do. Cast it, throw it off like casting the line out when you go fishing. Throw it out there, don't associate with it, don't spend time with it, don't take it in, and don't treat it like it's a normal part of life.

Just because everyone else is stressed out doesn't mean you have to be. There really is a better way to live life. The practical, everyday things God can handle all by Himself. No need to worry.

THE LOVE OF MONEY

First Timothy 6:10 tells us, *"For the love of money is a root of all kinds of evil, for which some have strayed from the faith in their greediness, and pierced themselves through with many sorrows."*

Whether you are already financially rich or whether you are in debt up to your eyeballs, riches are deceitful because they make promises they can't keep. Every promise in Christ is "Yes and Amen," but mammon masquerades as the answer to all our problems, appearing to be our provision to an abundant life. Riches can be deceitful because they promise us comfort, provision, and safety, therefore becoming an idol—a substitute for the true riches that can only be found in Christ.

Money is not the problem, but the love of money definitely is! Jesus related this fact to worship. Matthew 6:24 says, *"No one can serve* [worship] *two masters; for either he will hate the one and love the other, or else he will be loyal to the one and despise the other. You cannot serve* [worship] *God and mammon."*

Luke 16:14 tells us, *"Now the Pharisees, who were lovers of money, also heard all these things, and they derided Him."* That word for "derided" means they "turned their noses up"—at Jesus, really?!

Don't listen to the luring of riches. Listen to the Word of God. Serve Him! He is your Provider and He is faithful. Money is not your enemy; it is your servant, so never let it determine your assignment. Proverbs 10:22 says, *"The blessing of the Lord makes one rich, and He adds no sorrow with it."* That is amazing!

Love God and put your trust in Him. Don't be a lover of money—trust in true heavenly riches. Be a worshiper of the One who owns it all anyway!

THE DESIRE FOR OTHER THINGS

*But **seek first the kingdom of God and His righteousness**, and all these things shall be added to you. Therefore do not worry about tomorrow, for tomorrow will worry about its own things. Sufficient for the day is its own trouble* (Matthew 6:33-34).

Don't let the root of the desire for other things choke out the fruit of the Spirit. I think we need to be honest and ask ourselves these questions: "What do I want? What do I desire?" It's okay to desire a car or a house or whatever, but are you desiring God and His Kingdom first, or is God getting the leftovers? This is about living in the Spirit and walking in the Spirit. There has to be a balance between the spiritual and the natural, which is all rooted in priorities.

This is a big deal as it relates to our heart, and what a big deal our heart really is to God. Because our heart is like a garden, the soil of our heart determines how much of the seed of God's Word is produced through us and how we live out our days here on the earth.

Your heart matters and you must keep your soil in good condition. I can't do it for you and neither can anyone else. You are the one responsible for the ground of your own heart. Knowing how deeply loved you are, stay stirred up and motivated. Keep yourself in the love of God and consider Jesus often. Keep worshiping and investing into your relationship with Him so you don't become weary and discouraged in your soul.

Always know that, *"if you confess with your mouth the Lord Jesus and believe in your heart that God has raised Him from the dead, you will be saved"* (Romans 10:9).

8

DYING TO THE NATURAL, LIVING IN THE SUPERNATURAL

As mentioned in Chapter 5, a friend of mine and I were talking about being submitted to the plan of God no matter what, and he said, "This dying thing is killing me!" We laughed until we cried! Pressure doesn't create; it only reveals.

For example, when we lived in Oklahoma during the '80s, I learned that back then one of the ways they tested oil pipelines was by filling the newly constructed pipe with pressure from both sealed ends to see if the pipe was solid. It if wasn't, it would expose the flaws and the tiny, pinhole leaks. Pressure didn't create the leak, but it did reveal it.

Pressure can come from all kinds of situations. This being true, we sometimes feel like we are being squeezed from the inside out when in the midst of birthing something big, the midst of a big creative project, or honestly even just new circumstances.

Don't let yourself get stuck in something lifeless just because you're familiar with it or you're comfortable. Let God lead you into your new season. A trapeze artist has to let go of one bar to take hold of the next one. It would be impossible and foolish to try to hold on to both. There is a rhythm of grace, and the momentum of the Holy Spirit will lead you to the next season, the next assignment. When you hold steady through the resistance, you will experience breakthrough!

When you are in times of pressure or transition, don't check out; if you do, you won't get out! This is when you need to watch and pray! Be alert, watch, listen, and stay alert.

Our natural tendency is to do something—anything! The enemy knows this and tries to get us to act in fear or to prove we have what it takes. He did this with Jesus too. Matthew 4:1-11 tells us the story of when the enemy tried to get Jesus to do something! The devil wanted Jesus to turn stones into bread, jump off the highest point of the temple, and bow down and worship him. Of course, Jesus did none of what he asked. Instead, He quoted God's Word to him.

We have to labor to enter into His rest or we will labor at all the rest!

Hebrews 4:11 tells us how important it is to be diligent to enter into the rest of the Lord's finished works.

If you don't watch and pray, Jesus said we will enter into temptation, because even though the spirit is willing the flesh is weak. We can either enter into His rest or enter into temptation depending on our response to times of pressure.

On October 24, 1947, Chuck Yeager was the first person to exceed the speed of sound. Under immense pressure and the possibility of sudden death, he chose to reach his goal of breaking the sound barrier. When his plane began to shake, everything within him wanted to pull the throttle back. His natural instinct was telling him to pull back. Instead, he did the opposite and pushed the throttle all the way forward. As a result, he met even more resistance! The plane began to shake to the point that he thought it was going to fall apart. But rather than breaking up into little tiny pieces, the plane flew at 700 miles per hour, Mach 1, and broke the sound barrier. After that, the ride became as smooth as glass.

Hebrews 12:28 says, *"Therefore, since we are receiving a kingdom which cannot be shaken, let us have grace, by which we may serve God acceptably with reverence and godly fear."*

Don't feel like the process is unique to you—it's not. Jesus felt the pressure of the whole world on His shoulders when He was in the Garden of Gethsemane, near the Mount of Olives. The very word "Gethsemane" means "oil press" or a place of pressing. In the garden were ancient olive trees, and it was where Jesus and His disciples often went to pray (John 18:2).

The pressure we often feel in the midst of something new or something strategic about to happen is pressure against the soul. Even Jesus felt this, and He felt it like none other: *"Then He said to them, 'My soul is exceedingly sorrowful, even to death. Stay here and watch with Me'"* (Matthew 26:38).

Luke 22:44 says that Jesus was in such agony, that He prayed more earnestly, and His sweat was as *"great drops of blood falling down to the ground."*

Jesus says in John 5:30, *"I can of Myself do nothing. As I hear, I judge; and My judgment is righteous, because I do not seek My own will but the will of the Father who sent Me."* Clearly, we can see that Jesus had a choice. He had a will of His own just like we do. He was determined to not do His own thing but rather to do the will of the Father in every area of His life.

It is impossible for us to fully grasp what Jesus went through and the amount of intense pressure that He was dealing within in His soul to where he was actually sweating blood.

As we study this, we find that Jesus prayed the *same prayer* three times to bring His human soul into submission to the will of the Father. Verse 39 of Matthew 26 tells us Jesus said "the same words," and it took Jesus three times, as He was choosing to submit His "self" to the Word of God—refusing to allow His soul to be in control. Jesus was literally dying to His soul being in control before His body died on the cross. Wow!

We often don't think about the fact that Jesus was fully human as well as fully God. He prayed the prayer of consecration, submitting His will to the will of the Father, and it took Jesus three times that night to accomplish it (Matthew 26:36-46).

How many times will you have to take authority over your old thoughts and your self to submit your soul to the will of God?

Hebrews 12:3 says, *"For consider Him who endured such hostility from sinners against Himself, lest you become weary and discouraged in your souls."* The phrase "consider Him" means to focus on Jesus, to fix your thoughts on Him. The next time you feel that pressure, that shaking, that time of transition, don't become weary and discouraged in your soul; instead, take time *to consider Him* and watch what happens. Renewal and restoration! You are established on a foundation that cannot be shaken. So, as you behold Jesus, instead of shaking you can shake off what the enemy is trying to do and shake up his kingdom instead. Worship inside out!

GOD LOVED FIRST

I spent so many years trying so hard to love God with my whole heart! I wanted to love Him with my spirit, soul, and body; however, I knew inside myself that I really wasn't loving Him like that. I wanted to, but it seemed like the impossible dream. It wasn't until I realized how much He loved me that I had something to respond to. I was so focused on loving Him that I missed the part of Him loving me first!

Sometimes we're so busy moving forward we don't even know what we've left behind. I had attended many worship events telling me how I should love God with my whole heart. I knew Scriptures like Jude 21 that told me to "keep myself in the love of God" by praying in the Holy Spirit, and how important that was, especially in our generation—yet it wasn't until much later that I discovered how loved by God I really was, and how loved by God I really am. That changed everything.

One day while reading Ephesians 3:17-20, I realized that what Paul prayed for us was stunning! It's the first time I'd ever really seen it! He prayed that we would know the *love of Christ*, not the love *for* Christ. How had I missed that? I had spent so much time and energy trying to get enough love for the Father (see 1 John 3:1; 4:10; 4:19).

In other words, because Jesus appeased (satisfied) the wrath of God toward sin through His sacrifice for our sins in His own body on the cross, now we get to respond to His love by loving Him. We don't love Him so that He will love us back. God *is* love! Love was from God and is God's idea. God didn't love us back; He loved us first. Jesus laid down His life—literally His *psuche* (self), His soul—so we could have *zoe* (life), the very life of God. He wanted you!

STRATEGIC TIME

We are in a strategic time when many from former generations are wondering if we are ever going to see a move of God again, a revival, a renewal. Many of the young people don't have context because the Spirit of God has not been ministered in power and demonstration like the apostle Paul talked and wrote about. Many have heard things about it, but they have not seen it. In fact, I hear about it a lot from my students, and they are eager and hungry to see it!

It is always on the heart of God to connect generations and nations! How is He going to do it if He doesn't do it through you and me? Ignorance and captivity are never a blessing! When we hunger for the Word of God, we will find renewal and restoration. We are not waiting for God to move. *God is waiting for us to move in Him!*

There was a time in the Old Covenant when Israel was coming out of captivity to lay a foundation and rebuild. Some who had seen what once was wept, and others who saw what was brand-new shouted with great joy! The mixture of weeping and shouts of joy were heard in the same event.

> *And they sang responsively, praising and giving thanks to the Lord: "For He is good, for His mercy endures forever toward Israel." Then all the people shouted with a **great shout**, when they praised the Lord, **because the foundation of the house of the Lord was laid**. But many of the priests and Levites and heads of the fathers' houses, **old men who had seen the first temple, wept with a loud voice** when the foundation of this temple was laid before their eyes. Yet many shouted aloud for joy, so that the people **could not discern the noise of the shout of joy from the noise of the weeping of the people**, for the people shouted with a loud shout, and the sound was heard afar off* (Ezra 3:11-13).

I have had the awesome privilege of experiencing powerful moves of God and seeing the supernatural life of God bring supernatural results that were obvious to all. I have experienced the presence of God in such powerful ways that I didn't even know whether I was still here on the earth or not. I have tasted and seen the real thing, but as the years went on I have also been in many gatherings where there was no sense of the presence of God at all. I knew He was in us, but I just didn't sense any manifested presence from us at all. It was like we were content to just have Him abiding in us.

Experiencing the supernatural flow of God personally is the best, and it is for every believer. When you gather together and experience it on a corporate level, the joy is inexpressible and full of glory. No, really! It is full of glory.

But here is the challenge! Once you've experienced this kind of personal, powerful corporate worship where it is not just inspiring but transforming, it will spoil you forever. You will never want to go back to the lack of revelation and transformation. New wine can't go back into old wineskins. That is impossible!

Well, here is my encouragement to you. It's not supposed to! It's time for the matured men and women who have experienced spirit and truth to connect with the younger generations and demonstrate it! You can spend time crying over what once was, or you can sow some more seed, water what has been sown, and watch God give the increase so that both the sower and the harvester can rejoice together. God is even now connecting generations and nations!

Psalm 16:11 says, *"You will show me the path of life; in Your presence is fullness of joy; at Your right hand are pleasures forevermore."* In the presence of God is fullness of joy and being in the Word of God brings joy—again, showing us the value of life, not death. When we return to the Word of God, the Spirit of God agrees with it and with us, bringing us clarity and understanding. This releases tremendous joy that causes great rejoicing!

Later in the book of Nehemiah, after years of not ever hearing the Word of God publicly taught or preached due to their captivity, Ezra (God bless Ezra!) brings the Word before the whole assembly of men and women and he reads it from morning until midday. They couldn't get enough of it!

> *And Ezra opened the book in the sight of all the people, for he was standing above all the people* [on a platform of wood they made for this purpose]; *and when he opened it, all the people stood up. And Ezra blessed the Lord, the great God. Then all the people answered, "Amen, Amen!" while lifting up their hands. And they bowed their heads and worshiped the Lord with their faces to the ground* (Nehemiah 8:5-6).

The leadership helped the people understand the reading, and the people were so moved by the Word of God that *"all the people wept, when they heard the words of the Law"* (Nehemiah 8:9). Again, the leadership had to help the people not to sorrow or be grieved over what they had missed out on for all those years and rather to realize that this day was a new beginning, a day holy unto the Lord, and there was something special happening! They were instructed to go eat, drink, and rejoice greatly because they understood the words that were declared to them. It's a new season! Yes, we have to die to self, but we also have to enjoy the presence of the Lord as well.

JOY, PEACE, LOVE

The people were told, *"Do not sorrow, for the joy of the Lord is your strength"* (Nehemiah 8:10). Toward the end of the book of Nehemiah we read: *"Also that day they offered great sacrifices, and rejoiced, for God had made them rejoice with great joy; the women and the children also rejoiced, so that the joy of Jerusalem was heard afar off"* (Nehemiah 12:43).

I remember a time when we sang songs about the joy of the Lord, and they were usually up-tempo and bouncy. The overall impression was that we were supposed to try really hard to be joyful all the time; if we were, joy would be reflected in our faces. While this wasn't necessarily a bad thing, what we didn't understand about joy was that it was not a natural joy that we had to work up somehow. The joy of the Lord is a supernatural joy and is a beneficial result of the presence of God in believers' lives as new creations.

One day while reading in the book of Matthew a phrase of Scripture hit me like it was the first time I'd seen it! The end of Matthew 25:21 says, *"Enter into the joy of your lord."* In context, the entire verse reads: *"His lord said to him, 'Well done, good and faithful servant; you were faithful over a few things, I will make you ruler over many things. Enter into the joy of your lord.'"* Jesus was giving this lesson of the talents in parable form and was speaking of things in the natural that had a huge Kingdom, godly impact!

As I was reading and when I really saw that sentence, *"Enter into the joy of your lord,"* I immediately asked myself, *Why didn't I realize that we have to enter into the joy of the Lord? How do we enter into the joy of the Lord?*

Before we look at what the joy of the Lord is, we should probably first look at what joy is.

What is joy? The dictionary defines joy as an emotion: "The emotion evoked by well-being, success, or good fortune or by the prospect of possessing what one desires." Does this begin to show you why we don't understand what joy really is? The joy of the Lord is supernatural! For the unbeliever, joy is just an emotion at best and based on circumstances.

I had the lead role in the musical *Oklahoma!* when I was in high school. The lyrics of one of the well-known songs I sang were: "Oh what a beautiful mornin', oh what a beautiful day, I've got a beautiful feelin', everything's going my way!" I said, "Liar!" When has *everything* ever gone our way?

An unbeliever only knows joy as an emotion. A person not born again doesn't yet have the joy of the Lord. They don't know joy as a fruit of the Spirit, so it would be impossible for them to experience joy as a beneficial result of the Spirit of God.

Well then, what about peace, you might ask. Okay, what about it? The dictionary defines it as a state of tranquility or quiet, a freedom from disturbance. Really? In other words, we could say peace is a feeling. I feel peaceful or I don't feel peaceful, and it's based on being free from disturbance. This sounds nice, but it is so far below the life of God we live in Christ!

> *Now may the God of hope fill you with **all joy and peace** in believing, that you may abound in hope by the power of the Holy Spirit* (Romans 15:13).

Jesus says in John 14:27, *"Peace I leave with you, My peace I give to you; not as the world gives do I give to you. Let not your heart be troubled, neither let it be afraid."*

Paul tells us in Philippians 4:7, *"And the peace of God, which surpasses all understanding, will guard your hearts and minds through Christ Jesus."*

We have been given a peace inside that is greater than anything coming against us from the outside. In the midst of disturbance and chaos, we have a peace that is even more powerful—it's supernatural peace.

What about love? Again, just like joy and peace, the love of God is not natural; it is supernatural. God doesn't have love— God *is* love!

> *But God, who is rich in mercy, because of **His great love** with which **He loved us, even when we were dead in trespasses**, made us alive together with Christ (by grace you have been saved)* (Ephesians 2:4-5).

So clearly, all love is not the same love at all, is it? Love is not love! Sadly, lust is a more accurate term to describe what many today call love. In English, we use the word "love" for everything. We love God and pizza in the same sentence. I love my dog, I love my house, I love my car, I love God, etc.

God's love in the Greek language is the word *agape*, which is defined as the God kind of love.

> *For God **so loved** the world that He gave His only begotten Son, that whoever believes in Him should not perish but have everlasting life* (John 3:16).

For the believer, joy, peace, and love are not just emotions. Each will affect our emotions in a positive way, but in relation to the fruit of the Spirit, joy, peace, and love are reflections of the character of God—shining out through us.

The fruit of the Spirit is love, because God is love, and in this relationship with Love Himself we experience love, joy, peace, patience, kindness, goodness, faithfulness, gentleness, and self-control (Galatians 5:22-23).

There are several words for "joy" used in the original Greek, describing God's kind of joy, such as cheerfulness, calm delight, exceeding joy, to rejoice, to boast in or glory in, grace, the divine influence upon the heart and its reflection in life, including gratitude and liberality. Joy can also mean to jump for joy, exalt, and exultation. The joy that God gives us is a spiritual force that is constant from a calm delight to jumping for exceeding joy!

> ## The fruit of the Spirit is only produced by the Holy Spirit.

We have been translated from one kingdom (darkness) to another (light), from death to life, from the dominion of satan to the lordship of Jesus Christ. We can't let "dying to self" make us feel like we are killing ourselves. On the contrary:

> *He has delivered us from the power of darkness and conveyed us into the kingdom of the Son of **His love*** (Colossians 1:13).
>
> *For the kingdom of God is not eating and drinking, but **righteousness and peace and joy** in the Holy Spirit* (Romans 14:17).

Jesus said something very interesting in the following Scripture verse that will really bless you! Jesus said, *"These things I have spoken to you, that My joy may remain in you, and that your joy may be full"* (John 15:11). Why did Jesus specify *His joy* compared to *our joy?* What was His joy? Remember, the joy of the Lord is your strength.

> *Therefore we also, since we are surrounded by so great a cloud of witnesses, let us lay aside every weight, and the sin which so easily ensnares us, and let us run with endurance the race that is set before us, looking unto Jesus, the author and finisher of our faith, who **for the joy** that was set before Him endured the cross, despising he shame, and has sat down at the right hand of the throne of God* (Hebrews 12:1-2).

We already know from His experience in the Garden of Gethsemane that Jesus knew the price He was going to have to pay in being made sin on our behalf. He started paying that price within His human soul first. In the garden, He sweat blood over the agony of what was about to happen. He knew He could not let His human soul be in control. He knew He had to surrender in order to be in submission to pay the price that no one else could ever pay. The beating, the stripes, the crown of thorns, the physical torture were all part of what He went through on our behalf. Greater love has no Man than to lay down His life for His friends. Wait! Did the Son of God just call me a friend?

For He made Him who knew no sin to be sin for us,
that we might become the righteousness of God in Him
(2 Corinthians 5:21).

Trust me, Jesus was not jumping for joy that He was about to die on a cross. However, there was a calm delight inside as He knew the price of sin was being paid once and for all. He knew the price He was paying was priceless! He knew it was about you! I can just hear Him saying, "I'd rather die than be without you!"

We were the joy set before Him. His joy was having relationship with us. That was the calm delight that helped Him endure the cross. Of course it was hard—more than we can even imagine. Yet Jesus knew it was the Father's plan. He knew His obedience would open the gates of heaven for humanity to believe in Him and confess Jesus as Lord. The result—eternity together!

We were and are His joy!

Jesus already had a place with the Father, but what He didn't have was *you!* He had already heard the words from His Father, "You are My Son in whom I am well pleased." However, what He hadn't yet heard was your response to His love for you. Jesus endured the cross and the shame because of the joy that was set before Him—a relationship with you! Time with you for the rest of time! It's hard for us to really even begin to imagine what He went through to have us!

That's why now in this life, in this day and in this time, His joy is our strength. Our strength comes from our relationship with Him. Now in this life—not just when we get to heaven—now, because we are in the Kingdom of His dear Son, we can at any time and at all times enter into the joy of the Lord (Matthew 25:21).

We don't have to live our lives stressed out, with overloaded hearts, fearing our surrender to the Lord. He is working on our behalf even in our weakness. We are blessed because of what Jesus did for us, not because we sang a song or prayed a prayer! Because of what Jesus did, we can have a relationship and become a true worshiper.

In the middle of the storm, in the middle of the battle, we can count it all supernatural joy, peace, and love.

> *My brethren,* **count it all joy** *when you fall into various trials, knowing that the testing of your faith produces patience* (James 1:2-3).
>
> *And you became followers of us and of the Lord, having received the word in much affliction, with* **joy of the Holy Spirit** (1 Thessalonians 1:6).
>
> *In the world, you will have tribulation* [pressure, stress, adversity]; *but be of good cheer, I have overcome the world* (John 16:33).
>
> *For whatever is born of God overcomes the world. And this is the victory that has overcome the world—our faith* (1 John 5:4).

Fulfilling God's joy is being in relationship with Him and then with each other as a result. You can literally and freely give someone else what was freely given to you through Christ! Just like Peter and John did for the lame man at the temple gate called Beautiful, God wants to do something beautiful through you.

> *Then Peter said, "Silver and gold I do not have, but what I do have I give you: In the name of Jesus Christ of Nazareth, rise up and walk"* (Acts 3:6).

God's life in us is what makes us powerful. It certainly isn't us! We are not powerful, but even in our weakness He is powerful. His word is alive and powerful!

Philippians 2:13 says, *"For it is God who works in you both to will and to do for His good pleasure."*

His joy is our strength—for what? God wants us to be strong in Him, even when we feel weak in ourselves so we can endure hardships and overcome every obstacle, then help others do the same.

As children we are gathering together, taking our place to help serve in the Kingdom—and we do so with joy. The Holy Spirit of God was given to the church and the fruit of the Spirit is being manifested worldwide. Don't stand on the outside looking in. God wants to use you too!

> *The people who know their God shall be **strong**, and carry out great exploits* (Daniel 11:32).
> *That you may walk worthy of the Lord, fully pleas-ing Him, being fruitful in every good work and*

increasing in the knowledge of God; **strengthened** *with all might, according to His glorious power, for all patience and longsuffering* **with joy** (Colossians 1:10-11).

Finally, my brethren, **be strong** *in the Lord and in the power of His might* (Ephesians 6:10).

And the disciples were filled with **joy** *and with the Holy Spirit* (Acts 13:52).

Then the seventy **returned with joy,** *saying, "Lord, even the demons are subject to us in Your name." And He said to them, "I saw Satan fall like lightning from heaven. Behold, I give you the authority to trample on serpents and scorpions, and over all the power of the enemy, and nothing shall by any means hurt you. Nevertheless, do not rejoice in this, that the spirits are subject to you, but rather rejoice because your names are written in heaven"* (Luke 10:17-20).

Relationship with the Lord matters way more than what we do. What we do matters too. However, out of the being comes the doing, not the other way around. The 70 disciples to whom Jesus gave authority were pretty joyful over the ministry results they experienced. Jesus recognized the good fruit. However, He said the fruit was no comparison to relationship with Him. He was more excited about the root than the fruit! Those who are true worshipers are those who have a relationship with God in Christ; it's really that simple!

9

BEING FILLED

And do not be drunk with wine, in which is dissipation; but be filled with the Spirit, speaking to one another in psalms and hymns and spiritual songs, singing and making melody in your heart to the Lord (Ephesians 5:18-19).

But above all these things put on love, which is the bond of perfection. And let the peace of God rule in your hearts, to which also you were called in one body; and be thankful. Let the word of Christ dwell in you richly in all wisdom, teaching and admonishing one another in psalms and hymns and spiritual songs, singing with grace in your hearts to the Lord. And whatever you do in word or deed, do all in the name of the Lord Jesus, giving thanks to God the Father through Him (Colossians 3:14-17).

Again, we see the partnership between spirit and truth: *"be filled with the Spirit"* and *"let the Word of Christ dwell in you richly."* Jesus told us this was the only way to worship, and it is so true!

Notice these two passages point out that when the Word of Christ is living in us, then we can give to others by teaching, admonishing, and encouraging one another using psalms, hymns, and spiritual songs.

When the Word of Christ is dwelling richly in us, we will not be okay with lyrics that are contrary to the Word of God. If we wouldn't teach it from the pulpit, then why would we sing it from the stage? As a songwriter, I know the importance of writing lyrics that are aligned with the Word of God. Every lyric of every song must reflect the Word of Christ rather than conform to the ways of the world. Was that too subtle?

There are, in these two passages, three different kinds of songs. We are told that we can use each for a blended and balanced variety of music. The style of the music varies from culture to culture and from one era to another, but it is really just the platter on which to serve the lyrics. Make melody in your heart! Be creative and allow God to be glorified in you. This is not advice just for musical people. This is for every believer. You don't have to be a good singer to make melody in your heart to the Lord.

Let's take a closer look at these three categories of songs.

PSALMS

The word for "psalm" in the Greek is *psalmos,* which denotes a striking or a twitching with the fingers upon an instrument. We could say that a psalm is a song accompanied by a musical instrument. Many of the psalms from the book of Psalms were directed to God, and many of our modern songs that we sing directly to God are really psalms, too. Someone told me years ago, "Oh…you are called to be a psalmist!" I did not have a clue to what that meant. I thought it was someone who had to put everything into rhyme! However, a psalmist is someone who writes psalms. We typically refer to them today as songwriters. A psalmist is someone who can partner with the Holy Spirit spontaneously in a musical flow.

HYMNS

The Greek word for "hymn" is *humneo*. When I looked up the meaning of this word in Strong's Concordance years ago, initially I was not the least bit impressed: "to sing a religious ode or to celebrate God in song." Wow! I thought that is about as generic as I can imagine. When I asked the Holy Spirit to help me and lead me into truth, He showed me that the word "hymn" is only used in the New Covenant. It is not used in the Old Testament. When I studied more, I found that hymns contain the message of Christ—the gospel message, testimony, those kinds of things. Many of our "who we are in Christ" type songs would actually be hymns.

Matthew 26:30 says of the early believers, *"And when they had sung a hymn, they went out to the Mount of Olives."*

What is interesting for us in our culture today is we think hymns are songs contained in a hymnbook. I can guarantee you that Jesus did not have a hymnbook like we think of today. He did have the book of Psalms, which was kind of like their version of a hymnbook. It was a Jewish tradition to conclude the Passover meal by singing what was known as "the Hallel," which was part of Psalms 113–118. The content of these particular psalms has a huge emphasis regarding the Messiah and what would happen when Jesus became the sacrificial Lamb of God through being crucified.

It's important to realize that the New Testament writer didn't call what the disciples sang a psalm, even though it was from the book of Psalms! The writer, under the inspiration of the Holy Spirit, called it a hymn. It was on purpose to show us the New Covenant content. I would love to see more of this kind of song being used in the church today! We need to teach more doctrine and bring more New Covenant revelation about what Jesus did for us and who we are in Him.

SPIRITUAL SONGS

The words here for "spiritual song" in the Greek are *pneumatikos ode,* or a Spirit-inspired song to the glory of God. This kind of song was usually spontaneous and inspired right on the spot. It's interesting that in jazz music, there is a "go with the flow" kind of freedom, with improvisational and spontaneous moments that can be very exciting and inspiring. This is true of many styles, which makes me wonder—why aren't we seeing more of this in the music from the body of Christ? This was given to us. Why aren't we doing it? Why aren't we making room for this as well?

Instrumental music is beautiful. It can be improvisational or spontaneous; however, this category of "spiritual songs" mentioned in the passages from Ephesians and Colossians is referring to vocal music. This vocal music has lyrics, and when the Holy Spirit-inspired song comes it can be sung out as if it were coming from the people to God. This is usually represented by a solo vocalist in a public gathering. Then others join in on a phrase that repeats or a chorus that is easy to follow. It can also happen just between you and the Lord anytime or anywhere as you are worshiping Him in your day. The spiritual song can also be sung from the heart of God to His people, like a prophetic word in song. It will always be encouraging, uplifting, and will edify or build up the person hearing it. This is a Holy Spirit-inspired song, and when combined with psalms and hymns it can have a huge and dynamic impact on all.

HOW NOW SHALL WE LIVE?

Let me pose some thought-provoking questions:

- What would happen if we really learned how to live edified?
- What if we learned how to live every day built up in our spirit, worshiping from the inside out?
- What if we were being taught how to abound in thanksgiving and were being encouraged to express our praise to God?
- What if we were really abounding in thanksgiving and rejoicing evermore?
- What would our weekend gatherings be like if we were doing this on a personal, private level during the week?

Instead of being taught how to abound in thanksgiving, praise, and worship, many are being told to tone it down and be more accommodating—whatever that means. I'm not saying we should flaunt our liberty and be the center of attention in a corporate gathering, because that is just more self-centeredness being put on display. Rather, we should let the law of love supersede the law of liberty and allow people to grow, develop, and be discipled in worship, just like in any other area. This is what we need!

God gave grace a place, so why can't we? We should be *living to give* instead of *coming to get* in our gatherings as believers. We should be flowing together in agreement as doers of God's Word instead of settling for our opinions and preferences. We are not customers—we are believers!

> *And let us consider one another in order to **stir up love and good works**, not forsaking the assembling of ourselves together, as is the manner of some, but exhorting one another, and so much the more as you see the Day approaching* (Hebrews 10:24-25).

What would happen if we would take the time to sow into the Spirit, to minister to the Lord, and to build up and encourage our own souls in the Lord on a regular basis? I'm not saying that we don't need encouragement from each other; however, we need to first run to the throne and not to the phone!

Whenever the enemy tries to get you to shut up and not give thanks or not praise God, do the opposite! Turn it up and watch it turn around! Nothing can separate you from the love of God.

> *But you, beloved, **building yourselves up** on your most holy faith, **praying in the Holy Spirit,** keep yourselves in the love of God, looking for the mercy of our Lord Jesus Christ unto eternal life* (Jude 1:20-21).

Notice, we are the ones who need to build ourselves up! Life has a way of tearing you down, if you let it. Sadly, people put other people down all the time, and it can be very discouraging, especially when it comes from other believers. You'll sink to the bottom if you don't keep yourself stirred up! It's hard to edify someone else if you're not edified. As the Holy Spirit fills us, He flows out of us primarily in words. We speak, we sing, and we declare in the power of the Holy Spirit.

> *Therefore let us pursue the things which make for peace and the things by which one may **edify** another* (Romans 14:19).

Your soul needs to be built up upon your most holy faith, and one of the ways you can do it is by praying in other tongues—or what the Bible calls praying in the Holy Spirit.

> *For he who speaks in a tongue does not speak to men but to God, for no one understands him; however, **in the spirit** he speaks mysteries. …He who speaks in a tongue **edifies himself.** …For if I pray in a tongue, **my spirit prays,** but my understanding is unfruitful. What is the conclusion then? I will pray with the spirit, and I will also pray with the understanding. I will sing with the spirit, and I will also sing with the understanding. …For you indeed give thanks well*

[when you pray in the spirit].... *I thank my God I speak with tongues more than you all* (1 Corinthians 14:2,4,14-15,17-18).

This gift of speaking in tongues is exclusive to the worshipers of the New Covenant. No one in the Old Covenant could have spoken in tongues because the Spirit of God wasn't yet given to live inside of us.

John 7:38-39 tells us, *"He who believes in Me, as the Scripture has said, out of his heart will flow rivers of living water.' But this He spoke concerning the Spirit, whom those believing in Him would receive; for the Holy Spirit was not yet given, because Jesus was not yet glorified."*

When we are filled with the Spirit, what is inside us is supposed to be manifested outside for others to see His glory and believe.

> *And they were **all filled** with the Holy Spirit and began to speak with other tongues, as the Spirit gave them utterance* (Acts 2:4).
>
> *The gift of the Holy Spirit had been poured out...they heard them **speak with tongues and magnify God*** (Acts 10:45-46).
>
> *The Holy Spirit came upon them* [for the first time], *and they **spoke with tongues** and prophesied* (Acts 19:6).

Not only do we have the fruit of the Spirit available to us and manifested in our lives as revealed in Galatians 5:22-23, we also have the gifts of the Holy Spirit available today. We need to accept all that God has for us!

God has given us the gifts of the Holy Spirit to be a blessing through us to other people. We need them so much in our generation. Let's read what the Bible says about these gifts:

> *To another faith by the same Spirit, to another gifts of healings by the same Spirit, to another the working of miracles, to another prophecy, to another discerning of spirits, to another different kinds of tongues, to another the interpretation of tongues* (1 Corinthians 12:9-10).

God has given us supernatural ways of being built up. He intended us to live above the mundane and ordinary and live supernatural lives in a natural world.

So many churches have backed away from the things of the Spirit, including the gifts of the Holy Spirit. The church was born in the power of the Holy Spirit; therefore, how much more should we be manifesting and demonstrating these wonderful things from God!

The apostle Paul writes about ministering in *"demonstration of the Spirit and of power"* in 1 Corinthians 2:4. This is so important for our generation today. It should be our everyday lifestyle.

Paul told Timothy not to neglect the gift of the Holy Spirit that was in him and to not be ashamed or embarrassed, but instead *stir it up!* (See 1 Timothy 4:14 and 2 Timothy 1:6.)

More thought-provoking questions to consider:

- What would happen if we gathered together as believers already edified?

- What if we had been spending time in the Word, worshiping and praying, singing in tongues, prophesying to one another, and renewing our minds to the Word of God?

- What if we gathered to give what we have been given?

- What if there was space in our gatherings to do that?

- What if we came first to give and then to receive?

- What if in our worship gatherings—instead of just "empty space" stuff that doesn't really matter and isn't producing life—we allowed the Spirit of God to actually fill the space and manifest through us?

I believe most people gather together on a weekend for their own personal edification. I want you to be edified and so does every leader, I'm sure! However, why wait till the weekend service? Why aren't we living Spirit-filled on a daily basis?

Of course, there will be days when you will be living more filled than other days, truth be told; but still, the day to day was designed by God to be living in a place of more than enough. You may have been baptized in the Holy Spirit twenty years ago, but are you living filled with the Holy Spirit today? What would happen if we were living filled from day to day? We are to *be being filled,* always, every day! Then whenever we come together, we would have something to give instead of coming to get.

TRANSFORMATIONAL AND GENERATIONAL

If worship doesn't transform, is it really worship or just singing? Singing is amazing and awesome, but let's not call singing worship when it's really just singing. As the Bible says that love edifies while knowledge puffs up, knowledge is necessary to renew the mind; however, when knowledge is revealed to us by the Holy Spirit, it causes transformation, not just information. In the same way, worship is designed by God to be not just inspirational but transformational.

We transform from being self-centered to being God-centered and from wanting to be served and treated like a consumer to serving and acting like a disciple! Genuine worship is always life changing. Remember, self-will always seeks to impress, but the anointing seeks to bless! When we worship according to God's Word, it is already blessed. It contains the blessing!

> Self-will always seeks to impress, but the anointing seeks to bless!

Worship that is genuine always demands a response. When the young virgin Mary worshiped, she said, *"Let it be...according to your word"* (Luke 1:38). When John saw a vision of the risen Lord on the island of Patmos, he fell to the ground as if he were dead! (See Revelation 1:17.)

If worship becomes superficial and sentimental instead of worshiping in symphony with the Spirit of God, there will be nothing to respond to. Revelation demands a response! We need to fix our eyes on what is eternal (2 Corinthians 4:16-18). We should be experiencing the much more glorious!

As I was teaching my students recently about some of these things I've been talking about, I asked them if they thought it was true that their generation knows very little about the things of the Spirit of God, as well as moving in the super-natural both as a believer and as a leader in ministry. Solemnly they said, "Yes, that is true. We would love to see it, but no one is demonstrating what it looks and sounds like." That response made my eyes leak! I have such a passion to raise up this generation to learn how to live a lifestyle of worship inside out, while ministering in power and demonstration of the Holy Spirit! If we are going to *be being filled,* then we have a mandate to serve this generation with nothing less.

GENERATIONAL WORSHIP

Reaching generations has always been important to the heart of God. God's design is for us as worshipers to be connecting generations, not dividing them! What on earth does a "worship war" even mean? The Holy Spirit is the only One who can bring unity through the love of God. Yet somehow when we gather together, the family is divided up according to age. Then we wonder why the generations can't relate. Really?

> *For I have known him* [Abraham], *in order that he may command* **his children and his household**

after him, that they keep the way of the Lord, to do righteousness and justice, that the Lord may bring to Abraham what He has spoken to him (Genesis 18:19).

How great are His signs, and how mighty His wonders! His kingdom is an everlasting kingdom, and His dominion is from generation to generation (Daniel 4:3).

Tell your children about it, let your children tell their children, and their children another generation (Joel 1:3).

Give ear, O my people, to my law; incline your ears to the words of my mouth. I will open my mouth in a parable; I will utter dark [hard] *sayings of old, which we have heard and known, and our fathers have told us. We will not hide them from their children, telling to the generation to come the praises of the Lord, and His strength and His wonderful works that He has done* (Psalm 78:1-4).

The Holy Spirit is the connector of generations and brings unification, not segregation!

I understand that teaching on a level that can be understood becomes important to every age group. I even understand having times when they can worship in an age-related environment, which can have huge value. But! Can we have time corporately or publicly to worship together as a family, please? I want my grandkids to see me lifting my hands and praising the Lord—not just privately, but also publicly!

> *For by one Spirit we were all baptized into one body—whether Jews or Greeks, whether slaves or free—and have all been made to drink into one Spirit* (1 Corinthians 12:13).
>
> *For this reason I bow my knees to the Father of our Lord Jesus Christ, from whom the whole family in heaven and earth is named* (Ephesians 3:14-15).

We are members of the family of God and we all have a place at the table! Our blessing is that we are family, but you know what? Family is also our challenge, because no one chooses their family, do they?

This is why we need to be taught about generational connection! We now have four generations often represented in the same worship gathering. Therefore, if we make our worship about style instead of substance, we will cause more worship wars, more division, and more lack of fellowship!

Real people living real lives need a real God.

To everything there is a season! Our heart matters, time matters, and generations matter to the heart of God. We need to be being filled with the Spirit of God now more than ever! Many of our older generations feel like their church is no longer their church. The songs they loved are long gone, and, sadly, many times in the culture of the relevant what is being platformed is only the young and the beautiful. They feel like no one wants to hear their story or even associate with them.

On the other hand, our students are telling us that they would love to hear the stories of previous years and of those who have pioneered before them and helped to prepare their way. The young are often not the ones who are saying they don't want to hear from the older; in fact, it's just the opposite. It is often the older who don't want to stay involved with the younger generations. They feel like they've done their time and they would rather just stay retired. The problem with that kind of thinking is layered with obvious conclusions, but the bottom line is that in the Kingdom of God there is no retirement.

So I tell the older it's time to *refire!* I love to let them know that they are still valuable and that now more than ever we need spiritual moms and dads who are available to help connect the generations! There are so many young people who have orphaned hearts.

When Tracy and I were engaged and about to be married, she wisely asked my mom to share one of her most valuable life lessons with her. She was surprised to hear her say, "When you go into a crowded room and you don't know who to talk to, look for the oldest person there and strike up a conversation. Ask the person to share their story with you. You will learn from their experience, receive wisdom, and most likely find a generational connection." That was some good counsel!

God is a Gap-filler and a Way-maker! Everyone wants a place to belong, a place to be celebrated, not just tolerated. As one filled with the Spirit of God, you can also be a gap filler and be the place where authentic relationship can happen.

As the church, when the older learn to invest into the generations, the younger will learn how to value and honor their elders. We will come together to learn to smile on our future. We don't need to be conformed to the ways of the world and be discouraged by the way the world lives.

Many young people are filled with fear today because they are afraid of living, but they are more afraid of dying! This is why so many young people don't want to be around older people. They are afraid of their own mortality, and seeing someone older—especially those who are in their final years here on the earth—brings them face to face with their own future. Many are not ready to face it.

Let's change that sad scenario! Don't be so busy moving forward that you don't know what you left behind. All generations have value and vital contributions that can remove fears in every age group—when people connect. And what better place than at church—God's family together.

Older people need to feel valued for who they are and for what they have done in their lifetime. They need to know that they are valuable, that they have a story to tell that we want to hear and they have a place at the table. Let's be part of seeing honor restored. The Holy Spirit will help us. Worshipers love to give and they live to give.

Proverbs 23:22 tells us to *"Listen to your father who begot you, and do not despise your mother when she is old."*

And Psalm 71:18 says, *"Now also when I'm old and gray-headed, O God, do not forsake me, until I declare Your strength to this generation, your power to everyone who is to come."*

Also, 1 Timothy 5:1-2 says, *"Do not rebuke an older man, but exhort him as a father, younger men as brothers, older women as mothers, younger women as sisters, with all purity."*

Everyone in the family of God has a place at the table, which I see as a Thanksgiving table or a Christmas table where older people are loved, honored, and respected and younger people are loved, embraced, and celebrated as well.

How crazy would it be to tell Grandma to leave the table because she is no longer relevant, not cool anymore, or not as popular as she used to be! Our culture today is not geared to value the elderly, so we as the church need to show them what it looks like and how it works. We must learn how to spend time together, eating together, having meaningful conversations without a cell phone in one hand, and actually come together as the body of Christ!

If we really are a spiritual family, the family of God, then more than ever these family connections need to be taught—and caught! Show and tell! Be someone who shows it. Jesus tells us:

> *A new commandment I give to you, that you love one another; as I have loved you, that you also love one another. By this all will know that you are My disciples,* **if you have love for one another** (John 13:34-35).

How we love each other as the body of Christ is what speaks to the world. It shows that there really is something to our faith and that Jesus is Someone they want to follow as a result of seeing us as the body of Christ. They will know that you are a disciple of Jesus, not just a member of a social club.

Let's start loving each other as the church before we reach out to the unchurched. The harvest is already ripe, but the laborers are few. Let's change that too! We need to go out and go into all the world. Let's be worshipers who are also laborers. Let's be those who connect!

I hope I made it very clear in an earlier chapter that our heart matters, but my question to you now is—does God's heart matter to you? If it does, then generational connection will matter to you as well.

As believers we are being filled daily, even moment by moment with God's blessings, His Spirit, and the love of Christ Jesus.

> *Whom* [Jesus Christ] *having not seen you love. Though now you do not see Him,* **yet believing, you rejoice with joy inexpressible and full of glory,** *receiving the end of your faith—the salvation of your souls* (1 Peter 1:8-9).

10

THE UNFORCED RHYTHMS OF GRACE

[Jesus says,] *"Come to me. Get away with me and you'll recover your life. I'll show you how to take a real rest. Walk with me and work with me—watch how I do it. Learn the unforced rhythms of grace"* (Matthew 11:28-29 MSG).

Life is best lived with the unforced rhythms of grace.

Our existence here on earth in this realm of time is at best 120 years, right? So while we are here in a physical body, it is important that we learn how to live a balanced life, with our priorities lined up with Scripture, then live to the glory of God and not for our own self-satisfaction. God has blessed us to be a blessing. Learning to live yoked together with Him and live our lives in Him is vital to discovering life in the unforced rhythms of grace. Even our every heartbeat reminds us of rhythm.

From the earliest time I can remember, I felt rhythm in everything and thought everybody else did too. It wasn't until years later when I realized many of the sounds that I was hearing, others weren't hearing. The rhythms I was feeling were not always shared with the same fondness I was feeling, especially when those rhythms happened in church with me tapping all ten of my fingers on the top of the wooden pew in front of me while tapping both feet underneath me to rhythms that were begging for expression—even though we attended a traditional evangelical church with traditional church music!

I honestly can't imagine what I put my mom and my dad through, let alone my four siblings! I played drums on anything I could find—our old console radio with the oval glass covering the dials, alarm clocks with glass fronts, pots and pans—you get the picture. No wonder my parents finally got me a real drum. To no one's surprise, drums were the first of many instruments that I would learn to play growing up. It was like rhythm was in my blood, let alone my bones.

When I was in sixth grade, I sat next to a wall of windows on the east side of the classroom. In the morning, when I should have been focusing on math, my ears were tuned instead to the drum corps routines of the high school marching band that was practicing just outside the windows. It was almost torture for my body to sit in that classroom while my ears went on their daily march along with my head!

In about eight short weeks, I had memorized all twelve of their drum cadences and loved playing them at home on the snare drum that my parents had given me. The night they brought my younger brother home from his hospital birth, they gave gifts to each of us kids, along with the gift of their youngest of five. The drum was a marching snare drum, which I still have today.

One day after the high school concert band had rehearsed on the gym stage, I just happened to mention that I had memorized all the marching cadences to one of the drummers, a senior. She quickly challenged me to "Put up or shut up!" So, of course, I put up, and soon was asked with special permission to move up from the sixth-grade band to become the youngest member ever of the Drake, North Dakota marching band. I couldn't have been happier to finally have my ears, my head, and my heart marching to the beat of the same drummer!

For those who know me, that might explain a lot!

As I developed as a musician, I learned the value of "not rushing" the tempo and learning "groove" and what a difference the "bpm" (beats per minute) can make in the way music is made and music is received. I learned how complex and complicated rhythm can be, and how simple and relaxed it can be depending on how it is used. I began to see patterns that I somehow just knew were reflections of something deeper and more meaningful—what I now call the unforced rhythms of grace.

TIMES AND SEASONS

We are living in the time of grace—a new time and a new season to be spiritually new and to worship inside out!

Scripture has the following to say about times and seasons:

To everything **there is a season, a time for every purpose** *under heaven* (Ecclesiastes 3:1).

But as for me, I trust in You, O Lord; I say, "You are my God." **My times are in your hand**; *deliver me from the hand of my enemies, and from those who persecute me* (Psalm 31:14-15).

So teach us to **number our days**, *that we may gain a heart of wisdom* (Psalm 90:12).

Daniel answered and said: "Blessed be the name of God forever and ever, for wisdom and might are His. And **He changes the times and the seasons**; *He removes kings and raises up kings; He gives wisdom to the wise and knowledge to those who have understanding* (Daniel 2:20-21).

And He [Jesus] *said to them, "It is not for you to know* **times** [chronos] *or* **seasons** [kairos] *which the Father has put in His own authority. But you shall receive power* [dunamis] *when the Holy Spirit has come upon you; and you shall be witnesses to Me in Jerusalem, and in all Judea and Samaria, and to the end of the earth"* (Acts 1:7-8).

Be ready **in season** *and* **out of season** [to communicate the Word] (2 Timothy 4:2).

Time is valuable and we need to spend it wisely!

Seasons come and go here in Colorado where we live, and we love the changing seasons. We have seasons in our lifetime that change as well, don't we? We go through changes in life that for many include going from being single to married; having children, then grandchildren; from being younger to being older. I say "older" because my wife and I agreed that everyone is getting *older*, right? Even three-year-olds are getting older. We just decided to refuse to get *old!*

THE RHYTHM OF REST

As a musician, I have a good understanding of the value of a rest. I saw a cartoon recently showing a guy leaning up against a wall, under a sign above his head that had a quarter rest on the sign and a policeman telling him, "Sir, you are under a rest!" Okay, I know! Pretty corny and very "musician humor," but musicians don't just play the notes on the page, they have to play the rests as well for there to be the sound of music. It is true of life as well. God has given you a new song—for the *rest* of your life.

People today are so tired, stressed, and overcommitted—even fatigued. And yes, including believers—perhaps, especially believers? We're movers and shakers, right? Moving so fast, we don't think we have time to rest. I've personally heard people in my circle say, "I'll rest when I get to heaven!" Meaning it as a joke, kind of—but what's hiding underneath that statement? Could busy be masking something on a heart level?

Why do we often feel guilty if we rest? Why does rest seem so unnatural to us?

In John 9:4 Jesus says, *"I must work the works of Him who sent Me while it is day; the night is coming when no one can work."* I think ministers hear that and think we can never rest or take a break or even a vacation. But again, we need to look at the life of Jesus and see what He did. We are yoked together with Him and being led by His Spirit. We should not be driven and consumed with doing. You were never designed to be the only person going into all the world sharing the good news of the gospel. You are a member of the body of Christ, not the whole body. You are a person in a human body, and you need to be a good steward over the way you live, how you live—not just what you do.

Hebrews 13:9 says that *"it is good that the heart be established by grace."* We seem to be working harder and harder at trying to find quality of life. I have news for you! You're never going to find it by working harder. Jesus is the Author of quality life—life more abundant!

It is vital that we establish a foundation of "true rest" in our lives, where we have entered into the finished works of Jesus, so that our life can be established by grace and not by what we do.

> *There remains therefore **a rest** for the people of God. For he who has entered His rest has himself also ceased from his works as God did from His. Let us therefore be diligent to enter that **rest**, lest anyone fall according to the same example of disobedience* (Hebrews 4:9-11).

The King James Version of verse 11 says it this way: *"Let us labour therefore to enter into that rest."* While I was meditating on this one day, the Lord said this to me: *"Either you will labor to enter My rest, or you will labor at all the rest."*

God has called us to enter into the finished works of Jesus. What Jesus did for us is a finished work. We need to ask ourselves an honest question: "Am I trying or am I trusting?" Trust is based on a finished work. Trying is based on my own effort. Thinking my actions will qualify me to be good enough to deserve salvation and find the rest that my heart is longing for will lead me right back under the law. I will never be enough, and I will never have enough. Christ is enough and the finished work contains the rest we are craving.

Rest is the highest form of faith.

The rhythm of rest can become a lifestyle. The rhythm of rest is for the rest of your life! We who believe have entered His rest.

When you are really trusting in the promises of God as found in Christ, when you are believing God's Word and receiving by faith what He provided by grace, then there is rest. This rest has already been provided and you can rest in the promise of what God says in His Word. Unbelief keeps us from trusting, from resting in the finished works of Jesus. We often put more belief in the "woulda, coulda, shoulda," than in the promises of God. Hebrews 3:19 says, *"So we see that they could not enter in because of unbelief."*

Rest seems to get a bad rap by people who believe that if they are just strong enough, faithful enough, endure enough, and just keep pressing though, they can bypass rest and be among the elite who don't need to rest. They think rest is for the weak. We'll rest when we get to heaven. No, if we don't learn the rhythm of rest now, we may get to heaven even quicker than expected.

Who doesn't admire movers and shakers? I love being around the people I work with in ministry and have met some serious movers and shakers in my lifetime. I mean, who admires laziness and slothfulness? When someone is working 80 hours a week and is highlighted as the new shining star because of their long hours and commitment to fulfilling the vision, is it any wonder that a mere 40-hour work week seems pitiful? We wonder if rest is just wasting time and think that sleep is unproductive time.

Rest and sleep are not the same.

But Psalm 127:2 admonishes, *"It is vain for you to rise up early, to sit up late, to eat the bread of sorrows; for so He gives His beloved sleep."*

There are many studies revealing that many of us are surviving on four to six hours of sleep a night, and not good sleep at that. Sleep is vital to our well-being. Let's say in an ideal situation, sleep happens for eight hours; what about the rest of the day? Exactly! The rest of the day becomes the rest of your life, and as we learn to move into the unforced rhythms of grace and specifically the rhythm of rest, it will become a way of life.

When you are getting ready to go to sleep at night and you're lying in bed, instead of being on your phone or watching TV, spend time communing with the Lord. Psalm 4:4 says, *"Meditate within your heart on your bed, and be still."* And Psalm 63:6 says, *"When I remember You on my bed, I meditate on You in the night watches."* Devoting this time to the Lord before going to sleep is time well spent.

THE RHYTHM OF WORK

Unless a person is physically unable to work, there is never a good reason not to work. We need to see that our job and what we do matters. We must always do the very best job possible. There has to be a balance between being lazy and being a workaholic. I think most people struggle to find balance in life in various areas and live in the unforced rhythm of grace as it applies to work. Why is that rhythm so difficult? Why does it seem so complicated?

For years I thought work was the way, the source to make a living, and the goal was working to pay the bills and hopefully have something left over. We even define ourselves by our work. What we do for work has become our identity. Our doing has to come from our being and not the other way around! Years later, I discovered the following Scripture, which changed my perspective:

> *Let him who stole steal no longer, but rather let him labor, working with his hands what is good, **that he may have something to give** him who has need* (Ephesians 4:28).

231

We should have a banner over our heads, over our hearts, over our lives that reads: LIVE TO GIVE.

I had been in full-time ministry for years with international impact all to the glory of God. One of the most amazing things happened to me that helped me realize that even ministry is not who I was. I discovered in a whole new depth that, bottom line, who I was and who I am is a son of God, only because of Jesus.

In 2003 I moved back to Colorado Springs with the understanding that I had a full-time job in ministry at a large church in town. I had been in communication with the lead pastor, and I was instructed to "Just get back here"—only to discover that when I did, the full-time job was not communicated to anyone else so there were "no funds available" for that to happen.

After moving from several states away and moving into a house, I still had a calling—I just didn't have a job! I was no longer Daniel the worship leader or worship pastor or an associate pastor or even a senior pastor anymore. I had become unemployed Daniel. Thankfully, I had three offers at places for full-time employment without even saying anything to anyone. That was a blessing, but as I prayed about what to do I really felt the Lord say that we were not to move; we were to stay in Colorado Springs. It made no sense in the natural, but I put action to what I knew to do and didn't let what I didn't know stop me.

After further counsel from friends in ministry, I accepted a job working full time in a lighting showroom and became the sales manager within a few months. Then, after about a year, I started working two jobs. After I got off work at the lighting showroom at around 6 p.m., I quickly changed into construction clothing for my second job, working until around midnight. This second job was faux finishing, and I did that as self-employment for almost two years before going full time. It was a hard season and a lot of hard work. However, it was creative and my clients loved my work. I saw it as ministry and did it as unto the Lord. There were many times I would be praying for clients and God would give me a Bible verse to share with them. Sometimes I would write it on the wall in pencil before I began my faux finish over the top. I loved what I was doing even though it was very physically demanding work, especially for someone my age, but it helped keep me in shape.

Except for a small group event that I did once a month at our church, I was no longer leading worship, but I remained a worshiper often pouring my heart out to God alone on scaffolding high up in the air or working off a ladder, wondering if I was ever going to be in ministry again as a career. I remember wondering if this was similar to how David felt after he was anointed to be the next king of Israel yet returned to tend his father's sheep until God opened the doors of the new season.

There were many times when I had a feeling of loss, no longer leading people in worship publicly like I had for so many years. I had blessed so many in one setting, but now I was blessing one family at a time. Was the one less than the many in value to God? I adjusted my attitude by offloading my heart in worship over and over again, not knowing it was preparation for what was to come. I was grateful for the work and counted it all joy.

During this time, my wife and I went through some of the darkest times of our lives. It was my "dark night of the soul" for sure. Our senior leader fell into sexual sin and it became an international scandal, which had a huge and profound impact on me and on our family. If I would have been on staff, I would have been in the middle of it all. But God!

God had been protecting us all along, and what seemed like rejection was really protection! During one of my darkest days, I was in my home office paging through my Bible in frustration over everything that had happened and over what seemed to *not* be happening. As I was flipping through my Bible with my bad attitude, I heard the Spirit of God speak softly to my heart, calling me by name, "Daniel, you either believe this or you don't!" I turned some more pages and heard the same thing, but this time it was louder. Then, as I flipped a few more pages in frustration, I heard the Spirit again, but this time it was even louder, *"Daniel, you either believe My Word or you don't."* Then all of a sudden, in that moment, I stood up on my feet as I pounded my fist on the Bible, loudly proclaiming, *"I do believe!"*

As tears filled my eyes, I knew something had shifted! It was as if a switch was flipped inside of me from off to on! The hardness of heart that was trying to become my new normal melted away in that holy moment, and even though nothing had changed in my circumstances I knew everything had changed in my heart! I literally said out loud, "Oh devil, you have made a bad mistake! Not only are you *not* going to take what God has given to me, but God is going to raise up and restore and rebuild something that will impact the world! You'll see!"

That is exactly what happened!

Instead of teaching in a school of worship, God opened an opportunity that I would never have imagined in a thousand years—to start a school of worship instead! Andrew Wommack called me one day while I was faux finishing at a huge house. In the middle of my workday with paint and glazes all over my hands and face, and in the middle of my destiny being fulfilled, in that moment, through Andrew Wommack, God invited me into a whole new season with a job offer at Charis Bible College—to establish a School of Worship and a Healing School, as well as oversee the whole Charis Worship Ministry.

I will always be grateful to God and to Andrew Wommack for giving me an opportunity to do what I'm doing. I love the work I do here! At first, I was hired to oversee three areas. Several years later I was officially overseeing seven areas of ministry and loving all of it. The ministry was awesome and I felt so blessed. One year we decided to do three completely different Christmas Dinner Theater events back to back on consecutive weekends. It was so much work, but we did it! Then to my surprise, I hit the wall! After working out, I was on my way from the garage into the house and could barely make it up the stairs. A family friend is a naturopathic doctor, and my wife insisted I get checked out, so I did. He told me my adrenal glands were completely depleted and I was in a dangerous spot. If I would do nothing but rest, I would potentially start to recover. No work, no nothing—just rest. It was one of the hardest things I had ever done. It felt like such a waste of time!

Consequently, I learned an important lesson about finding the unforced rhythms of grace in my work, not because I didn't like it but because I loved it! I was determined to go the long haul, so I learned from this setback and found the balance in my life I was missing.

Maybe you can relate? Maybe like me you are on the edge of burnout or maybe have nothing left to give because your body is declaring, "Enough already!" This is classic behavior of someone who is driven! It might feel like you're being led to take on more and more, but most likely it's a disguise for being driven.

People who are driven usually only feel good about themselves when they are accomplishing something. They look for more and more things to accomplish. It's like the adrenaline rush from working out becomes an adrenaline rush from doing more and more—and it becomes addictive. It is hard for driven people to enjoy what they already have and already have accomplished ; because they are so busy moving forward, they find it almost impossible to live in the present. It's a fine line and one that usually gets blurred. These people get things done, but at what cost?

God wants us to be diligent, not driven. There is a big difference.

THE RHYTHM OF PLAY

Did you know there was a commandment that says, "Thou shall not have fun; neither shall you smile, laugh, or have a good time"? Me neither! Thankfully there never was one, although I've been around people who must think there is one!

Have you been around believers who are really serious about life and about fulfilling the great commission to the point that there is no time to have fun? Play and fun to them is a waste of time. These are usually the driven type and have never thought of including play as a part of their goals.

I've often said it is no fun at all to be around believers who look as though they have been baptized in pickle juice instead of being baptized in the Holy Spirit. They are such sourpusses!

Listen, don't get me wrong—there is a lot about life that is serious. There are wars and rumors of wars, people starving, believers being persecuted and killed for their faith, and all kinds of evil throughout the world that we cannot ignore, pretend it isn't there, or not care. However, we don't have to bring the care of all that into our homes every night and burden our spouse and our children with all the depressing news of current events and what has gone wrong during the day.

When you are in ministry as a career, it's easy to make your table discussion centered on what went wrong with the day or discuss your office discussions with your family, most of which they don't need or want to know. Protect the atmosphere of your home—make it a safe place, a place where everyone can relax and have a good time. Yes to responsibility and yes to standards, but don't try to save the whole world at the dinner table.

Sadly, many people don't really know how to relax. Rest? What is that? Hobbies? What for? You know the type. The goal of play is to have fun! Play should not have a goal other than enjoyment.

My grandchildren love to hike and explore. Our home backs up to 150 acres of wildlife reserve, right in the middle of Colorado Springs. It's great! As we are hiking, it's amazing what comes out in the conversation. I imagine that it might have been similar with Adam and Eve in the garden as they walked and talked with God in the cool of the day. Usually there is no agenda, although there have been times when there was something specific that needed to be said, so instead of "going behind the barn," we did it on a walk. Usually the conversation is purely spontaneous, which is what makes it so much fun. Whatever the age, it's a safe place to unload their hearts, know they are still loved, and that they have a place called home.

Then there is family play. It could include activities like hiking and exploring, but with younger children it's fun to play board games, go to the playground, and go on vacations together, like camping. I remember Dr. James Dobson saying years ago that camping was the best possible family vacation for true relational connection. You can plan a fun family night doing something that the family enjoys. We had family nights with our kids from the time they were little. Some were more successful than others, of course, but the goal was always to enjoy the time together with each other.

Our granddaughters still talk about when Papa would sit on the floor and play tea party, usually with pretend tea and cookies. They would use their imagination to create scenes and conversations that often erupted into laughter and just pure silliness. Other times it was quite formal; we learned about manners and why they mattered. I was the minister guy in a suit on stage at church, but to my granddaughters I was in my lounge pants and a t-shirt, lying on the floor covered with stuffed animals and tea things. It wasn't wasted time—it was invested time.

When it's time to play, do it with all that is within you! Be present and enjoy it instead of wishing it was over. If you're waiting to play until your work is all caught up, you and your family will always be waiting. There will always be work and deadlines to meet. As someone's life is coming to a close, I have heard so many times how they wish they had enjoyed their close relationships more, learned to love more, to laugh more, and to enjoy life more.

THE RHYTHM OF WORSHIP

As I write, I realize that it has been four years since I started this book! I thought I was going to have it done in a few months, but here I am, four years later, and only now finishing the last part of this last chapter tonight. I am wondering what impact this book will make and whether my desire to not write not just another book about worship was realized or not. I really wanted you to understand that our worship is no longer from the outside in, but rather from the inside out—unforced grace as the motivator.

We are the place where the presence of God is abiding. We've been brought into a face-to-face relationship that is twenty-four hours a day, every day. It's not just a brief encounter like it was with Jacob in the Old Covenant. He said of his encounter: *"For I have seen God face to face, and my life is preserved"* [spared] (Genesis 32:30).

God told Moses, *"You cannot see My face; for no man shall see Me, and live"* (Exodus 33:20). But you and I can experience a face-to-face relationship with Him every day. What a treasure! What a gift! Jesus said that a face-to-face, Spirit-to-spirit relationship is how we *must* worship. Do you realize what a privilege this is?

I have often wondered what it was like when Noah built the ark, when David killed Goliath, when the walls of Jericho came tumbling down, when the temple of Solomon was filled with the glory of God, and when fire came down from heaven on the sacrifice of Baal and consumed the very stones of the sacrifice. I have said several times, "I can't wait until I get to heaven and I can ask them!" However, do you know what's going to happen? They are going to interrupt us, and say something like, "Oh that was amazing, and we will tell you about it; but first, would you please tell us what it was like to have the Holy Spirit living inside you? Would you tell us what it was like to have 24-7 access to God Himself and to be able to worship from the inside out in Spirit and in truth? Please tell us about it! What was it like?"

Worship puts everything in perspective! I'm so glad that God is God and I'm not! Self-centeredness can't stand when in the presence of God. When Jesus becomes our focus instead of self, a new perspective takes over unlike anything available to us in this life.

Ultimately, worship isn't something you can read about in a book; it is something you've been called into as a lifestyle. Worship is meant to be experienced. It's lived inside out! When we have a face-to-face relationship with God as Father, because of Jesus, of course, doesn't it make sense that we are family? Jesus came to reveal God as Father because we are family!

If we don't understand this close-knit family relationship, then we become part of a corporation or a mission or a cause, and while each of these things has a measure of truth, they cannot be the foundation upon which we build our lives.

We are the church, and we are family! Because of this, our relationship with God gives us relationship with one another. As the body of Christ, we are connected. This is why the presence of God now living inside us can be expressed through relationship; this is how we can have fellowship with one another.

In the early church, Acts 2:42-47 tells us there was a supernatural connection that manifested as a result of the Holy Spirit within the believers. The vertical and the horizontal come together to show forth a crucified life. Thank God for the cross and the resurrection!

That which was from the beginning, which we have heard, which we have seen with our eyes, which we have looked upon, and our hands have handled, concerning the Word of life—the life was manifested, and we have seen, and bear witness, and declare to you that eternal life which was with the Father and was manifested to us—that which we have seen and heard *we declare to you, that you also may have **fellowship** with us; and truly our **fellowship** is with the Father and with His Son Jesus Christ* (1 John 1:1-3).

*The **grace** of the Lord Jesus Christ, and the **love** of God, and the **communion** of the Holy Spirit **be with you all**. Amen* (2 Corinthians 13:14).

When Tracy and I were married in 1977, we were married in a historic, beautiful Baptist church where my dad was serving as pastor in Alamosa, Colorado. There were many people getting baptized in the Holy Spirit, and many youth were coming to the church. The whole dynamic of the church began to change. We were family and we were small enough to actually have meaningful relationships. When someone had a need, we usually knew about it and did something about it. We were connected, we were for each other, and we wanted to be a blessing to one another.

No one was striving to launch their worldwide ministry and no one was soliciting partners from another ministry's database. No one saw themselves in competition with another ministry, let alone each other. There was no "my ministry is bigger than your ministry" happening because we were all ministering in ways that would not have made headlines, but it sure mattered to the people who were doing the giving and to the people who were receiving.

People were getting saved, people were getting Spirit-filled, and people were being healed—lots of people were getting healed. But you know what still is talked about to this day? The love expressed in small ways that were full of big impact.

The times together in fellowship when we shared a meal and prayed together. We studied the Word together, but we also helped each other repair cars, fix broken stuff, or suggested where it could be fixed. We delivered meals when babies were brought home from the hospital, and when young wives needed advice the older women helped them and showed them what to do. The same was true with the younger men and the older men. There was a family connection and a rhythm of worship packed with compassion. We saw what we were doing as worship!

You know what? It was worship! This was the intention of God connecting us as family in the first place. It was His design that we so loved each other that the world would take notice, seeing that we were disciples who had been hanging around Jesus.

> *Now when they saw the boldness of Peter and John, and perceived that they were uneducated and untrained men, they marveled. And **they realized that they had been with Jesus** (Acts 4:13).*

Finding the rhythm of worship in the unforced rhythms of grace finds the heartbeat of God Himself being expressed in the everyday, the ordinary—turning ordinary into extraordinary and natural into supernatural. It's a touch, a smile, a cash gift, a prayer; sometimes it's food or a cup of water. Often, it's laying hands on the sick or visiting someone in prison. It's reaching out to those who have never heard the gospel and loving them enough to show them the love of Jesus before telling them about Him.

As a husband how I love my wife, and as a dad how I love my children, and now as a papa how I love my grandchildren

The rhythm of worship in the unforced rhythms of grace finds the heartbeat of God.

are all connected in relationship and expressed in love as worship unto the Lord.

Enjoying what God has created and finding joy in the smallest of things in nature and giving Him glory is worship! Giving Him glory for all the grand sunsets and sunrises on a daily basis and the fresh air and the mountain majesty surrounding us here in Colorado is such a joy! What was He thinking when He made all of this for us? Wow!

All of our thanksgiving becomes worship unto God as we respond to Him loving us first, long before we were anywhere around. The creation is wonderful, but how much more the Creator! We don't worship the creation, but we certainly do worship the Creator and thank Him for what He gave to us and all He has done for us! His glory is everywhere! What a joy to share it with others!

When the Son of Man comes in His glory, and all the holy angels with Him, then He will sit on the throne of His glory. All the nations will be gathered before Him, and He will separate them one from another, as a shepherd divides his sheep from the goats. And He will set the sheep on His right hand, but the goats on the left. Then the King will say to those on His right hand, "Come, you blessed of My Father, inherit the kingdom prepared for you from the foundation of the world; for I was hungry and you gave Me food; I was thirsty and you gave Me drink; I was a stranger and you took Me in; I was naked and you clothed Me; I was sick and you visited Me; I was in prison and you came to Me."

Then the righteous will answer Him, saying, "Lord, when did we see You hungry and feed You, or thirsty and give You drink? When did we see You a stranger and take You in, or naked and clothe You? Or when did we see You sick, or in prison, and come to You?"

*And the King will answer and say to them, "Assuredly, I say to you, inasmuch **as you did it to one of the least of these** My brethren, **you did it to Me**"* (Matthew 25:31-40).

We don't have to worship to get the presence, we worship from the presence. Now through being connected to the Head of the body of Christ, Jesus, that same place of His presence can flow from life to life and from heart to heart as we stay face to face and worship inside out.

CLOSING PRAYER FOR A NEW BEGINNING

*Father, thank You in Jesus' name for personally revealing Yourself to me. Jesus, You came to the earth to show us the Father! I want to see You as **the One who is greater in me** than he that is in the world! I want to see You high and lifted up! The One who is great and greatly to be praised. Thank You for sending the Holy Spirit to live in me.*

Thank You for personally leading me into all truth and even showing me things to come. Thank You for revealing any area of my life where I have been believing a lie. Show me what the life of a worshiper looks like for me, now, in this season of my life. Thank You for living in me and flowing out from me in rivers of living water and showing forth Your salvation from day to day.

Help me to see how all of my life matters and all of it fits together in Your life. I want to embrace being in You so much that my life is no longer my life. It's in You I live and move and have my being. Thank You for helping me to always glorify You in my body and with all that is within me. Thank You for helping me see the revelation that You designed my body to be Your temple while I am here on the earth.

*Thank You for teaching me how to manifest Your life through my life, my heart, my hands, and especially my mouth! Thank You for helping me, Holy Spirit, to be being filled with you and not with all the other things competing for my attention and my affection. I seek You first and Your Kingdom **first**, not last! Thank You for making me in Your image and teaching me how to worship in spirit and truth. Thank You for my new identity in Christ and for the authority and the power in Jesus' name to worship inside out!*

ABOUT THE AUTHOR

Daniel Amstutz is a seasoned, ordained minister who has served as a pastor, associate pastor, and primarily as a worship leader for more than forty years. He is president of Daniel Amstutz Collective, Inc. and is passionate to see the balance of Spirit and truth and the revelation of New Covenant worship impact the body of Christ.

Daniel is also on the faculty of Charis Bible College in Woodland Park, Colorado, where he serves as the director of the Charis Worship Ministry, the School of Worship Arts, and is the director of the Healing School. He holds a Bachelor of Music degree from the University of Colorado in vocal performance and Bachelor of Theology degree from Christian Life School of Theology. He is a published author, songwriter, and recording artist.

Daniel and Tracy have been married for 43 years and have two grown children and seven grandchildren.

Connect with us on

Facebook @ HarrisonHousePublishers

and Instagram @ HarrisonHousePublishing

so you can stay up to date with news

about our books and our authors.

Visit us at **www.harrisonhouse.com**

for a complete product listing as well as

monthly specials for wholesale distribution.

The Harrison House Vision

Proclaiming the truth and the power
of the Gospel of Jesus Christ with excellence.
Challenging Christians
to live victoriously,
grow spiritually,
know God intimately.